A COMPLETE GUIDE TO ENSURING A SUCCESSFUL BUSINESS

How to Begin, Survive and Thrive in the Competitive Market Environment

DR YUBRAJ GIRI

authorHOUSE

AuthorHouse™ UK
1663 Liberty Drive
Bloomington, IN 47403 USA
www.authorhouse.co.uk
Phone: 0800 047 8203 (Domestic TFN)
+44 1908 723714 (International)

© 2019 Dr Yubraj Giri. All rights reserved.

No part of this book may be reproduced, stored in a retrieval system, or transmitted by any means without the written permission of the author.

Published by AuthorHouse 12/02/2019

ISBN: 978-1-7283-9608-8 (sc)
ISBN: 978-1-7283-9607-1 (hc)
ISBN: 978-1-7283-9609-5 (e)

Print information available on the last page.

Any people depicted in stock imagery provided by Getty Images are models, and such images are being used for illustrative purposes only.
Certain stock imagery © Getty Images.

This book is printed on acid-free paper.

Because of the dynamic nature of the Internet, any web addresses or links contained in this book may have changed since publication and may no longer be valid. The views expressed in this work are solely those of the author and do not necessarily reflect the views of the publisher, and the publisher hereby disclaims any responsibility for them.

CONTENTS

Foreword xi
Foreword xiii
Preface xv

Chapter 1: An Introduction to Business 1
  1.1. What is Business? 1
  1.2. Key Business Activities 2
      1.2.1. Accounting 3
      1.2.2. Finance 3
      1.2.3. Human Resource Management 4
      1.2.4. Manufacturing 4
      1.2.5. Market Research 5
      1.2.6. Product Development 5
      1.2.7. Marketing 6
      1.2.8. Purchasing and Selling 6
  1.3. Business History 7
      1.3.1. Relationship between Money and Business 7
      1.3.2. Evolution of Money 8
      1.3.3. Evolution of Business 9
      1.3.4. Industrial Revolution - Background and Impacts 15
      1.3.5. Recent Trends of the Business 22
  1.4. Types of Businesses 27
      1.4.1. Sole Proprietorship 27
      1.4.2. Partnership 28
      1.4.3. Limited Partnership 29
      1.4.4. Corporation 30

  1.4.5. Limited Liability Company 31
  1.4.6. Non-profit Organisation 31
  1.4.7. Co-operative 32
  1.4.8. Franchises 32
 1.5. Public and Private Companies 34
 1.6. Difference between Public Companies and Public Sectors .. 36

Chapter 2: Beginning a Business - Key Procedures 37
 2.1. Market Research 37
  2.1.1. Data 38
 2.2. Data Analysis Techniques 42
  2.2.1. Qualitative Data Analysis Techniques 43
  2.2.2. Quantitative Data Analysis Techniques 49
  2.2.3. Mixed Data Analysis Techniques 52
 2.3. Understanding Consumer Behaviour 53
  2.3.1. Influence in Consumer Behaviour 54
  2.3.2. Consumer Buying Behaviour Process 56
 2.4. Market Segmentation and Targeting 58
  2.4.1. Demographic Segmentation 59
  2.4.2. Behavioural Segmentation 60
  2.4.3. Psychographic Segmentation 60
  2.4.4. Geographic Segmentation 61
 2.5. Selection of Products/Services 61
  2.5.1. Identification of the Target Market 62
  2.5.2. Market Research 63
  2.5.3. Selection of Products/services 63
  2.5.4. Product Test 64
  2.5.5. Improvement as Required 64
 2.6. Aim and Objectives 65
 2.7. Resources 68
  2.7.1. Financial Resources 68
  2.7.2. Human Resources 72
 2.8. Sources of Finance 72
  2.8.1. Internal Source 73
  2.8.2. External Source 76

2.9. Determining a Suitable Source of Finance 80
   2.9.1. Type of Business 80
   2.9.2. Required Amount 80
   2.9.3. Purpose 81
   2.9.4. Time Factor 81

Chapter 3:   Thriving in the Competitive Market Environment 82
   3.1. Customers are the Business Hub 82
   3.2. Competitive Strategies 83
      3.2.1. Porter's Competitive Strategies 83
      3.2.2. Gray and Balmer's (1998) Corporate Identity 88
   3.3. Competitive Advantage Components 90
      3.3.1. Financial Abilities 91
      3.3.2. Human Resource Management (HRM) 91
      3.3.3. Supply Chain Management (SCM) 92
      3.3.4. Product and Service Quality 94
      3.3.5. Technology 95
      3.3.6. Infrastructures 95
      3.3.7. Marketing 96
   3.4. The Marketing Mix 96
      3.4.1. Product 98
      3.4.2. Price 99
      3.4.3. Place 107
      3.4.4. Promotion 112
      3.4.5. People 131
      3.4.6. Process 135
      3.4.7. Physical Evidence 140
   3.5. Effective Planning 142
   3.6. Execution of Planning 143
   3.7. Use of Stakeholders' Feedback 144
   3.8. Research and Development 145
      3.8.1. Synthesising Information 147
      3.8.2. Data Presentation and Hypothesizing 147
      3.8.3. Data Analysis 147
      3.8.4. Design, Develop, Test and Improvement 148

  3.9. Perpetual Changes 148
  3.10. Adequate Financial Resources 149

Chapter 4: Business Growth and Develop 150
  4.1. Thrive Objectives 150
  4.2. Growth Strategies 151
    4.2.1. Market Penetration 152
    4.2.2. Market Development 152
    4.2.3. Product Development 153
    4.2.4. Diversification 153
  4.3. Growth Monitoring 154
  4.4. Sustaining the Business Growth 154
    4.4.1. Employees' Talent 155
    4.4.2. Effective and Efficient Operation 155
    4.4.3. Selection of Right Target Market 156
    4.4.4. Right Decision at Right Time 156
    4.4.5. Great Leadership 156
    4.4.6. Risk-Taking Ability 157

References 161

LIST OF FIGURES

Figure 1: Key business activities 2
Figure 2: Maslow's hierarchy need 55
Figure 3: Consumer buying behaviour process 56
Figure 4: Competitive advantage 84
Figure 5: Components of the competitive advantage 91
Figure 6: Supply chain management (SCM) process 92
Figure 7: 7Ps of marketing mix 98
Figure 8: Price-demand relationship in price skimming strategy 102
Figure 9: Components of the promotional mix 112
Figure 10: Globally spent amount in advertising (in billion
             US dollar) 118
Figure 11: Types of Public Relation 121
Figure 12: Different forms of direct marketing 125
Figure 13: People's role in different sectors 132
Figure 14: Research and development cycle 146
Figure 15: Ansoff matrix 152

FOREWORD

Through this book, the author Yubraj Giri provides a guide for organisations which are not successful on how to captivate, grow and sustain in a competitive market as well as those that are trying to enter the market. The book also discusses essential business components and offers effective and efficient suggestions on operating an organisation. The author with his intensive research in the field of business understands the vital component that goes into any business. He explains in his own words how failure though inevitable may be irrelevant as it goes through logical and systematic business process.

The book can be useful for those interested in business and secure a sustainable competitive advantage. This book discusses the essential information related to business in simple terms.

Dr Prakash Raj Malla

FOREWORD

In his first book publication, *'A Complete Guide to Ensuring A Successful Business : How to Begin, Survive And Thrive in the Competitive Market Environment'*, Yubraj Giri makes good attempt to provide a simplistic view of business and its elements for the benefit of any newcomer reader discovering the world of business. Whilst this book is not based on any empirical research in its own right, the author seems to have put together core concepts of business management, and offered useful insights into the ways of running a successful business. As a non-expert reader in the field, I find the book useful, and I believe this could be used as a reference material by students and practitioners engaged in the field of business management. I would like to congratulate Yubraj for this publication and I wish him all the best for his future endeavours.

Dr Krishna Adhikari
Oxford University

PREFACE

As a researcher, I have involved in the business management field for a decade and got an opportunity to minutely evaluate every core component of the business. Also, while assessing the business cases, I have found that several organisations have been failure in fulfilling strategic objectives which has created a bizarre situation in the business sector. Considering the fact, I have realised that I have to share my knowledge and assist the businesses which are being failure or the people who are trying to enter into the business but do not have adequate idea.

This book introduces the major aspects that are required to establish, sustain and grow a business. It presents every topic in simple and straight forward way; so, it can be easily understood by everyone. It introduces business and identifies the processes to establish, succeed, sustain and grow in the competitive market environment. It entirely guides a person to be a successful entrepreneur. Also, it can be used in the academic sector by the business management students and professors as the reference book.

With an immense devotion and motivation, I have accomplished this dream project. While writing the book, I have got an emotional, psychological and economic support from my dear wife (Mrs Shanti Giri), to whom I am extremely obliged. Without her support, I could not accomplish this book. Also, I would like to remember my dear parents, who are the light of my education. Finally, my sincere gratitude goes to everyone who has directly or indirectly contributed to get this work done.

CHAPTER 1

An Introduction to Business

1.1. What is Business?

Business is a bundle of commercial activities which are typically profit-oriented. Venugopal (2006) defines business as "all the activities concerned with production, manufacturing, lending, selling, leasing and the like, for earning profit." It tries to justify that business is not merely selling the products and services as customarily understood. Business is an art, and as such, its success depends upon the skills and abilities of a management team that handles overall business performance to fulfil its strategic objectives. Some people might have an inherited business skill. For instance, the Newari communities in Nepal have better business skills, but these skills alone may not be sufficient to fulfil business objectives in the competitive market environment. Every business person should acknowledge relevant strategies, be aware of new technologies, conduct market research, and have suitable experience.

Business activities are different from other activities as they are profit-oriented. If someone is working to support others devoid of any profit earning intention, such activities come under social or charity work rather than business. There are several organisations which are working not for profit but charity. For instance, Oxfam stores in high street in the UK sell products including clothes, foods and decoration items to raise finance for needy people in the world. There is no profit generating interest; so, these activities do not come under business activities. But if a child often purchases sweets from the supermarket and sells to his class-mates at a higher price, this activity becomes a business activity.

Also, all business activities should add value to the products or services. For example, a corner store sells grocery products to the customers at the convenient area. And the customers happily pay something more compared to the price at the supermarkets. Here, being convenient is adding products' value.

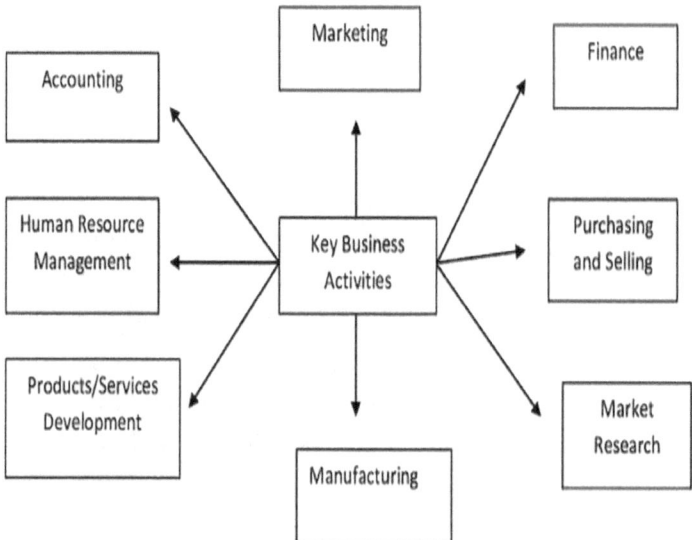

Figure 1: Key business activities

1.2. Key Business Activities

Every business organisation can have various activities which can be categorised under eight significant sectors like accounting, finance, human resource management, manufacturing, market research, product development, marketing, and purchasing and selling (figure 1). Each sector has to coordinate with others and add value to the products and services. Every business activity has to be guided by the strategic aims and objectives of the organisation. Business activity is like a teamwork in which if any action does not go properly; the entire business will be negatively affected.

1.2.1. Accounting

Accounting is the process of collecting and reporting financial information. As it depicts the financial position of a business, management can easily understand the strengths and weaknesses in financial activities. Such acknowledgement gives management a golden opportunity to diminish flaws and enhance opportunities in fulfilling financial objectives. Everett, Johnson and Madden (2012) define accounting as an amalgamation of different financial entities such as assets, liabilities, revenues, expenditures and fund balance elements. In other words, it is a commercial language that communicates an organisation's financial health to its stakeholders.

Every business has its financial transactions that the accounting department systematically records, analyses, monitors, and reports (Chikuhwa, 2013). Whether it is a small or big business, these activities are important. But some of the small business organisations may lack adequate knowledge and finance required for thorough application. It does not mean that they completely ignore accounting activities. Although they do not have written or formal accounting, they remember, calculate and analyse key financial data, and come to a conclusion. Such accounting information might be tentative but it outlines an overall financial information and facilitates to improve future financial activities.

1.2.2. Finance

Finance refers to the allocation of assets and liabilities to fulfil particular aims and objectives of an organisation. Sometimes, it can be understood as synonymous with investment, because in a business, money management indicates the process of generating income. Of course, an investor invests money to get a better return. There might be several potential areas of investment, and out of which an investor has to select the most suitable or profitable sector(s) to which evaluation of financial information is important. Also, to effectively operate a business organisation, basic financial understanding is required because it identifies "your financial options and limitations." (Argenti, 2012) It indicates that finance is the heart of any business organisation.

1.2.3. Human Resource Management

Human resource management (HRM) has key responsibility for managing employees, including selecting and recruiting, offering training and development programs, motivating employees, communicating targets, and conducting employees' performance appraisal. In most of the bigger organisations, there is a separate HRM department, but smaller organisations may not have (Machado, 2013). An organisation might have several resources which are used by human resources or employees to create product value. In this regard, the more employees are skilful, motivated, enthusiastic, hard-working, innovative, optimistic and result-oriented, the better value can be created. The HRM is responsible for ensuring these attributes in its employees and fulfilling strategic objectives of the organisation.

1.2.4. Manufacturing

Manufacturing is a process of producing products by exploiting raw materials, human resources, and technologies. According to Dahotre and Harimkar (2008), "Manufacturing refers to the processes of converting the raw materials into useful products." Of course, it uses various raw materials as the nature of the products. Some people believe that manufacturing is the process of producing a bulk amount of products using machines or new technologies. But according to Groover (2010), producing large quantities of products is manufacturing where is no mandatory use of machine or technology. If the product is innovative and that better fulfils needs and desires of the target customers, it can be popular and easily achieve competitive advantage. While manufacturing a product, customers' needs and desires become the key concern. If the product cannot address target customers' needs and desires, they do not buy it, and the business become failure in fulfilling strategic objectives.

1.2.5. Market Research

Market research indicates to collecting and analysing information about the target market. According to Clow and Stevens (2009), market research "refers to procedures and techniques involved in the design, data collection, analysis, and presentation of information used in making marketing decision." Market research helps to make marketing decision related to 7 Ps of marketing mix - price, promotion, product/service, place, process, physical environment and people. It allows an organisation an opportunity to acknowledge the market and assist in achieving competitive advantage. If an organisation does not comprehend the market, it cannot identify customers' expectations, determine suitable price and select better means of communication.

1.2.6. Product Development

Without a suitable product, an organisation cannot sustain in the competitive market environment. Product development is a continuous process throughout the life of business because along with alteration in the target market's needs and desires, an organisation should bring adjustment in its product features (Ward and Sobek, 2014). If an organisation cannot be able to fulfil the expectations of the target market, it is impossible to increase customer, revenue, and profitability. Without suitable products, an organisation cannot be successful in fulfilling its strategic objectives. Market research can be used to understand the target consumer behaviours. To develop the most suitable products an organisation has to consider the findings of the market research. Then, the products should be tested in the sample target market to identify any flaws and make improvements before sending them in the market.

1.2.7. Marketing

Producing better products or services is not enough for a business to succeed in a competitive market environment. An organisation has to make target customers aware of the products and encourage them to make a buying decision to which marketing is essential. Marketing is an activity of promoting products through the means of advertising, sales promotion, personal selling, public relation and direct marketing. Reynolds and Lancaster (2007) define marketing as an amalgamation of several techniques that are applied to market the products and services. It also helps to determine suitable marketing mix strategies.

1.2.8. Purchasing and Selling

As the nature of business, goods or products might be different, but the activities of purchasing and selling are essentially involved in every business. Some of the companies purchase finished goods or services and sell at a higher price in the market, but some others buy raw materials and manufacture products to sell in the market (Kotler, Burton and Deans, 2015). Purchasing is a vital component of the business activity as it involves selection of the most suitable products or services. For instance, to produce tasty and quality chicken item, McDonald's needs to purchase fresh and healthy chicken. If it cannot outsource quality raw chicken, it cannot produce tasty and quality chicken products. While purchasing and selling, every organisation has to consider facets like quality, quantity, delivery time and price. A business produces products or services for the customers; so that, selling higher quantity and satisfying customers can be the substantial objectives. Marketing strategy strongly supports selling products and services. The more customers satisfy or have trust in the products, the more an organisation can increase its sales and brand reputation. Also, unique products or services that better fulfil customers' needs and desires can be easy to sell in the market.

1.3. Business History

There is no actual beginning date of the business as it has existed for thousands of years in different forms, unlike the modern business. Even in the primitive age, people used to exchange goods and services for fulfilling their needs and desires, but they are not recorded. To make business more comfortable, people invented money, and it has a close relationship with the evolution of the money.

1.3.1. Relationship between Money and Business

The history of business can be somehow related to the history of money. In the past, money indicated to anything that was commonly accepted by the group of people to exchange products, services and resources. Before the invention of money, there was bartering system - an exchange of goods or services as per required. Exchanging a bucket of wheat with a bucket of rice can be a good example of bartering. Issues related to determining worth of various products and carrying them from one place to another made it difficult to practise in day to day life. People realised the necessity of money, and subsequently, they invented. Now there are several currencies which can be easily calculated or exchanged as per the value. For example, the value of 1 pound sterling is higher (approximately 1.40 cents) than the US dollar.

According to Pailwar (2011), in the past, along with bartering, different commodities were also used as money. They used cattle, seeds, tea, and many other commodities as money. But they had barriers like difficulty to store for a long time, carry from one place to another and determine the actual value. To resolve these problems, they invented coin and paper money that replaced commodity money. But it could not completely replace bartering which is still in practice in some of the villages. Around 5000 BC, people started to use money as the form of metal objects (Abdul, 2009). It means to say that at that period, metal objects were used to represent money and around 700 BC coin replaced metal objects in the western world. They gave a certain value of the coin, and it was used to buy goods and services. Then, in 960 AD, ancient China first introduced paper money since a big amount of coin money became difficult to carry from one place to another (Davies, 2010).

Carrying a big amount of money is risky as it can be lost or stolen; thereby, people developed the concept of electronic banking in the later phase (Schaechter, 2002). Through the means of electronic banking, people can easily and securely complete any financial transaction. Now, almost everywhere in the world, online transaction is in practice that saves time and effort as well (Asifulla, 2016). Further, in later days, digital currencies called Cryptocurrency are in practice. Although it does not have any physical or tangible existence, it is an asset, and people can exchange its value with physical currencies.

If people did not invent money, it was impossible to see business in this current developed and modern form. It means to say that business rapidly flourished at optimum level across the world along with the invention of money. Business organisations would use commodity money as it would have a problem in storage as well as valuation. So, people would not be interested in selling their products; they would produce products only for their uses but not for selling purpose. If someone in the neighbour needs, then it would be exchanged or purchased using commodity money or metal objects. So, business would be still in the primitive age if there would not be money.

1.3.2. Evolution of Money

As mentioned already, business history is closely associated with the history of money; thereby, it is essential to review a short evolution of the money. In the beginning (before 10,000 BC) people practised barter which was the exchange of resources (plants, cattle and crops) in a mutual understanding. It used to be applied merely to fulfil individual or family needs and desires (Andrei, 2011). The resources further expanded to different livestock, grains and plants in between 9,000 BC and 2,000 BC. Around 1,200 BC, people began to use cowries which was the shells of mollusc and would be available in Pacific and Indian Ocean to exchange goods and services instead of bartering practice (Weatherford, 2009). Further, around in 1,000 BC China introduced the first metal money, which was in the form of knife and spade (Cheock, 2017). Later, different other countries also adopted it and used in various shapes and forms. Then, around 500 BC, the modern coin was developed out of the silver in Lydia. The modern coins were made of valuable metals, including gold, bronze and silver (Howgego, 2002). Similarly, in 118 BC, China made leather money which was one foot square large. Through its inspiration in 806, China made the first paper money (Lopus, 2013). And at present, people are using different forms of money like coin, paper money, cheque, bank transfer, digital currency, and bartering as well.

1.3.3. Evolution of Business

In the absence of record, it is tricky to say exactly when the first business started in the history of human civilisation. Before 700 AD, businesses might not have functioned as the company; so that, their activities were not recorded in the business history; they remained on the lap of uncovered history. Guinness World Records claims that Nishiyama Onsen Keiunkan - a hot spring hotel - is the oldest business company in the world. It was established in 705 AD, and by the time of 960 AD, joint company and partnership (which are the foundations of the modern capital structure) concepts were established in the market (Zhang, 2014). For the long term, such types of companies remained in smaller scale due to lack of suitable market, poor economic situation and low quantity of production. During the Medieval period (from 5th to 15th century), there was neither competition nor any gluttony of earning profit. Also, there was no legal boundaries set by the government to operate, regulate and systemize the business (Wilson, Toms and Jong, 2016). The businesses used to be governed by ethics and mutual understandings. As they were not authentically profit-oriented companies, there was no unhealthy competition. At the time, the value of the product was very high due to the lower production and higher market demand. So, the businesses did not have any problem in selling the products unlike at present.

In the 16th and 17th centuries, business became more competitive, and it was used as a tool to gain power, respect and prestige; so, at that period, international trade was swiftly developed (Moens, 2003). Different governments, including the British government and the Spanish government, started international trade as the weapon to collect power and colonise countries. They used to sell stocks and bonds by establishing companies in the local territories (Amatori and Jones, 2003). At that period, British East India Company and Dutch captured most of the world economy; so, they became politically powerful in the world. To reduce the distribution cost and quick delivery, they started to use steamboats. They used telegraph communications, urbanisation and machines in making effective communication, better distribution and proper fulfilment of the target market's demand (Hoover, 1992). They started systematic and modern management to succeed in their aims and objectives; thereby, professionals were used to manage the organisation (Amatori and Colli, 2013). During that period, mercantilism was popular in Europe. Mercantilism is the theory used to believe that a country can be wealthy and powerful through exporting goods and collecting precious materials like gold and silver. England was the centre of the mercantilism due to the massive British Empire (Magnusson, 2015).

To prevent British colonies from outsourcing foreign goods, the British government introduced some acts, including Navigations Act (1651) and the Sugar Act (1764). It restricted colonies from buying foreign products; thereby, it simply created a monopoly in selling its products at a higher price and accumulated the national wealth. The Navigation Act (1651) restricted foreign vessels in using export products through its colonial coasts. They could engage in the colonial coasts only after getting pass through the British trade control officers. As England imposed the act, it was made difficult to import any products directly from the foreign countries. By such control, it was accumulating more wealth and increasing numbers of colonies. The Sugar Act (1764) introduced high customs for imported sugar and molasses from any foreign countries except than the colonies of England and British. It made imported sugar and molasses more expensive; thereby, they could not compete in British colonial markets (Stone, 2013). France, Spain and Portugal were also competing with the British government to increase their wealth and colonies around the world.

In the 19th century, numbers of reputed business organisations including Proctor and Gamble (1837), The Bethlehem Steel Corporation (1857), New York Condensed Milk Company (1857) and Coca Cola Company (1887) were established (Grant, 2005). By the end of the 19th century, many governments developed different rules and regulations to control, monitor and systematise business organisations. Most of those rules focused on trade balance between countries and earning international currencies (Lee, 2016). In the 19th century, several railroad companies were established in the United States of America. They are understood as the first modern management companies to set employees' terms and conditions which contributed to clarifying employees' roles, responsibilities and benefits. Also, they adopted accounting principles to effectively record and manage the account (Clark, 2004). Afterwards, companies like Singer and Marshall Field began their promotion (marketing) in the target market to get more construction contracts and increase profitability (Goddard, 2011). If there were few companies, promotion might not be crucial, but along with the increased competition in mid of the 19th century, promotion became an inevitable aspect of the business. During the century, Europe continuously produced different commodities, including oil, steel and rubbers, and exported to different countries through advanced ocean freights. Since then, every professionally managed business organisations started to recruit employees in managerial positions as well. It signifies that they have realised the importance of effective business management to beat the increasing competition (Grant, 2005).

Industrial revolution (1770-1914) was the key foundation of the modern business because at that time guild-like shreni, partnership, joint-stock companies and merchant collectives were successfully practised. These types of business trends have been continued by this time, but in developed forms as the governments have set clear laws and regulations to control and monitor the performance. In the past, ethics and mutual understanding used to guide those businesses but now the encoded business regulations direct their activities to make fairer, easier and more effective. The revolution brought a drastic change in the business along with rapid growth in industrial products, use of machine and change in business tradition. It began from the United Kingdom, and then spread to other parts of Europe as well as to the United States of America (Allen, 2009).

In the 20th century, especially during the First World War (1914-1918) industries related to automobile, aviation, communication, weapon, electricity and petroleum were significantly flourished, and they experienced a kind of breakthrough in the businesses. During the First World War and its aftermath, many governments spent much money in the weapon industries; so, that period remained unproductive for the rest of the business types. After the war, business was about to wake up but shortly the Second World War (1939-1945) began and except the above mentioned few types of industries, others extremely suffered and most of them shut down (Jeremy, 1998). Aftermath of those two world wars, business began its smooth development. In the 1950s, there was rapid growth and development of construction industries, military and allied industries, petroleum industries, broadcasting media and transportation. In the 1960s, airline industry got a significant rise, and the government developed businesses laws and regulations to systematise their activities and develop further. In the 1970s computer was invented, and the businesses entered into modernity. In the 1980s, business organisations introduced mobile phones, medical technologies, biotechnologies and information technologies (Jeremy, 1998).

In the 1950s, the motorcycle industry was highly flourished in different countries, for example in the UK BSA, Norton and Triumph, Italy Moto-Guzzi and the United States of America Harley Davidson. Honda's contribution is also equally important in the history of the motorcycle industry. In 1946, Honda company was established in Japan and began its manufacturing since 1949 from Alaska. By 1964, it established as a world-leading motorcycle manufacturing company (Brown, 1998). By adopting an aggressive sales distribution channel, Honda became able to control world's motorcycle market. But later on, Yamaha and Suzuki companies challenged it targeting the young generation. It is notable to say that in the 1950s, Japanese companies were not good enough to produce quality products due to lack of technology. So, they started to buy technology licence from different foreign companies and started to produce automobiles and electronic products; that is the reason, by the 1960s, they become world-leading companies (Shimokawa, 1994).

Some of the Japanese companies such as Matsushita, Toshiba, Hitachi, Mitsubishi, Sony, Sanyo, Seiko, Citizen, Orient, Fujifilm, Nikon and Casio were the most renowned in the second half of the 20th century. Similarly, American companies like Bethlehem Steel, US Rubber, General Motor, Eastman Kodak, Shell Oil, Ford Motor, Boeing, Apple and Microsoft, became the most renowned companies of that century (Forbes, 2017). Aftermath of the Second World War, business developed considerably in different other countries, including in the UK, France and Germany. As a result, the business transformed to the advanced stage at present.

In the 1970s, business encountered with a type of chaos that broke new idea into the modern business. Scholars like Michael Jensen attacked on corporation to release the unused or trapped assets to boost the business. As an organisation becomes able to utilise the trapped assets, further opportunities can be easily created (Shaw and Barry, 2015). Also, to reduce the company's debts and increase profits, the new idea encouraged the organisations to offer extra incentives to the managers. At that time, the governments introduced tax which increased managers' burden in reducing operation cost and earning better profit. By that time, several local and international business organisations emerged across the world that increased competition; thereby, the business organisations paid more attention in developing business strategies (Blackford, 2012). Organisations' new situation shifted managers' share primacy to the development of necessary skills and abilities on managers. Every organisation started to focus on developing leadership skills, managerial skills and business strategies. During the 1970s, management in every company remained under pressure due to rapid changes in customers' expectations, new technology and market competition.

But the business could not keep on continue in its development race as expected because of a great economic recession in the 1980s. It was due to increasing inflation and interest rate, and decreasing employment rate and purchasing power of the customers. During the recession, several countries remained in high debt, and they became unable to run their public services. To get rid of the recession, different governments gave much emphasis on deregulation and privatisation (Grusky, Western and Wimer, 2011). Due to this focus, computer technology got in light which replaced the typewriters. Also, the personal computers allowed people to store and retrieve information easily. Steadily, different business organisations adapted it one after another, which created a new hope to the business organisations (Stoltman, 2018).

The 1990s remained as a foundation of mass technologies as it brought a great revolution towards mechanical application in business organisations. Several businesses started to use digital systems that made their operations more effective and efficient. Information and technology sector developed rapidly and speedily, which made communication easier and more effective. Also, it strengthened the concept of globalisation. Although the internet was introduced in the 1980s to transfer and receive information in the academic sectors, it became accessible to the general public in the 1990s (Ceruzzi and Aspray, 2003). As soon as it was accessible to the public, the concept of e-commerce was also emerged and gradually brought into practice. E-commerce made customers easier to do shopping as they could search and order products online. Similarly, in the 1980s, banks introduced the internet banking system, but it got popularity in the 1990s (Cronin, 1998). Due to this system, e-commerce become much more easier and effective.

In the beginning of the 2000s, the business environment factors strongly supported the growth and development of the business, but at the end of the decade, the world slumped into a terrible economic recession. As a result, several organisations shut down their businesses, and some of them declared bankruptcy. Industries related to housing, retail, banking and hotel were badly affected at that time (Bailey and Chapain, 2012). Besides, major cities in the world suffered from terror attacks. On 11th September 2001, the World Trade Centre in New York was attacked by al-Qaeda that killed over 3,000 people and damaged infrastructures over $10 billion (Gard, 2002). Such attack intensified global worries in business investment and growth. The future of the business remained uncertain; thereby, the business activities declined, including innovation, market development and product development. But several social media like YouTube, Facebook, Instagram and Twitter emerged as the hope, and they helped to effectively promote the products and services in the target market (Brossman and McGaha, 2011). Also, the rapid development of technology replaced old technologies and converted the world into the digital planet.

According to Hunter (2013), in the 2010s, the world became able to recover from the economic recession. In the rise of economy and rapid development of information technology, business optimised its potentialities.

1.3.4. Industrial Revolution - Background and Impacts

1.3.4.1. What is Industrial Revolution?

The phrase "industrial revolution" consists of two words - "industrial" and "revolution" - where industrial indicates to the mass production by using machines in the factory and revolution designates to a sudden change. It tries to suggest severe change in the production system compared to the past (Wrigley, 2010). Before the industrial revolution, just a small quantity of products used to be produced fully depending on human resources instead of using any machine, unlike at present. But during that period industries developed various new machines to increase the quantity of products. Those machines brought a significant shift in the business focus from product centre to customer centre. Since machines produced a large quantity of products, the business organisations started to find more customers and earn more profit (Kotler, Burton and Deans, 2015). Until the industrial revolution, the major focus was on producing a large quantity of products, but after that period customer attraction, satisfaction and retention have remained key concerns of the business. Currently, the products are easily available in the market, and the customers have a bundle of choices. If the customers do not like the products, they do not buy it; thereby, while developing a product customers' needs and desires turn out to be the major focus. Industrial revolution has two stages:

1. The first stage (1770-1870) focused on steam, water, iron and a shift from agriculture to industry;
2. The second stage (1870-1914) emphasised on the development of new technologies, electricity, petrol engine, oil, and steal (McNeese, 2002).

During the first stage (1770-1870), several reputed businesses were founded for example, by the 1790s, Wedgwood firms were established aiming to process and increase the standard of the hand-made tea (Hobsbawm, 1977). They began to produce a large quantity of tea, and for its aggressive sales, they emphasized on its branding and marketing aspects. They well organised the business by recruiting employees' outside the family members and each employee was assigned a particular task (Makdisi, 2007). They manufactured mass products to earn more profit. Similarly, in the 1830s, several railroad companies emerged, which were supposed to have first modern management companies (Wilson, 1995). During that stage, construction-related organisations were highly popular in Europe.

In the beginning of the second stage (1970-1914), founder lead companies had a monopoly. But in the 1900s, they were replaced by professional management companies which were run either by the executive director or the externally recruited managers (Wood, 2002). Subsequently, the manager became a career in the history of business; the managers used to apply their skills and abilities to succeed in organisations' strategic objectives. But along with increasing competitions, managers required extra effort and to compensate, the organisations started to offer them an investment opportunity. If the managers also invest in the same business, they could better explore their optimum potentialities.

1.3.4.2. Background of Industrial Revolution

Industrial Revolution began along with the agricultural revolution (17th - 19th century) that attempted to increase the quantity of product and decrease the amount of labour cost. During that time, the major focus of the farmers would be to solve existing famine problem (Kerridge, 2013). Although the farmers used to work hard, the production would not be that much. At that time, issues like poor productivity of the land, ineffective harvesting system, primitive storage, and fully depending on manual effort were the major problems of agriculture (Kerridge, 2013). Also, there was low food production, and on the other hand, the population was continuously increasing. The food price was also very high that increased the wealth of the aristocratic class, but the lower-class people struggled to survive from the starvation. This circumstance amplified the necessity of agricultural revolution.

The agricultural revolution has a great contribution to end centuries-long traditional mode of production. It brought several reforms, for example, firstly, the small cut off pieces of lands were combined into a large plot. Secondly, based on suitability test, new crops were planted. The crops that fit to particular soil could produce more products. Thirdly, to identify new and better crops for the higher fertility rate, people started to research soil test, irrigation and hybridisation (Kerridge, 2013). In different seasons, the farmers used to produce various crops. Fourthly, they started to convert small lands into large plots because large and structured plots would have better productivity in lesser labour effort. They barred plots to save crops from castles and wild animals. And fifthly, they introduced machine and new technologies to save farmers' time and effort. That agricultural revolution significantly reduced the importance of the peasants. Also, it contributed to make landlords richer and working-class people poorer, which increased an economic gap in the society. In the past, the landlords used to produce low quantity of food, but due to the agricultural revolution, the quantity was increased, and the labour cost was decreased. Also, it remarkably reduced the number of peasants; thereby, farming jobs were also decreased (Luxemburg, 2012).

In pre-industrial Revolution, European society was static and guided by privilege culture where the aristocratic people would have an ultimate power in society. At that time, people used to gain power through the means of infrastructures like land and food processing mills. Also, people used to take cattle as a significant source of earning power and reputation (O'Brien and Quinault, 1993). The poor class people had to work hard in aristocratic people's farm to join their hands and mouth. They were not free in making their decision; they used to work as slaves of the aristocratic families. Season and the landowner used to determine their lifestyle. They should be guided based on the seasons and direction of the landowners. Besides, the Lords used to impose labour tax on those working-class people. The collected tax would be used to build some public infrastructures, including roads, dams and windmills (Crone, 2015). The pre-industrial society used to give a higher priority to the craftsmen and their positions would also be higher than the peasants (Goloboy, 2008). Guilds, professional organisations, used to set standard, price, wages, rules and regulations related to the artisans. Also, those organisations would be responsible for some of the social welfare activities, including looking after craftsman's family if he dies early. At that time, the merchant would be classified as the aristocratic group, which would be economically and politically powerful in the society. Along with the rise of the Industrial Revolution, that group became more active in producing and selling goods in the market. Before the Industrial Revolution, that group used to earn money by moving products from one place to another. But during the Industrial Revolution, they got significant political power that helped them to develop business and earn more profit (Cipolla, 2004).

1.3.4.3. Impacts of Industrial Revolution

Industrial Revolution has a significant impact on economic and cultural sectors. It increased material wealth which made people's life easier. Also, it restructured social trends from primitive agricultural-based rural society to industry-based urban society. Such society gave much importance to materialistic prosperity. Besides, it contributed to rapid urbanisation and established industrial employment culture. Industries focused on developing employees' skills and abilities to increase the product quantity. At that time, employees were valued and respected in the society (Conkin, 2008). Previously people used to work as the peasants for particular landlord in the household environment. But the Industrial Revolution abolished peasant-lord relationship and established a new workers-merchants relationship. The aristocratic people held industries in which workers had to work under strict rules and regulations. Most of the work structures were changed from outdoor to indoor, but it was not easy because the employees had to work hard and fast pace with the machine. Adult males used to work over twelve hours a day and six days a week. Working under high pressure with machine and long working hours increased the productivity of the industry (King and Timmins, 2001). Industrial revolution mainly affected in the Western world, where it brought a great change in agriculture system and everyday life environment. The productivity during the period was the second-highest increase in the world. The highest increase took place during the Neolithic Revolution around 10,000 BC, when the community became less nomadic and started to rely on agriculture and animal husbandry (Allen, 2009).

In the agricultural economic model, the role of female would be only to support male members, but the Industrial Revolution broadened their roles to the industrial jobs (Burnette, 2008). The industries used to recruit females in the low skilled and low paid jobs, but they had to make hard effort. At that time, males would have a significant role in the decision-making process. The females were given more job; they had to work over ten hours in the factory and had to complete all household activities. Including in economic resources, women were deprived of political and social rights (Burnette, 2008). Also, in the agricultural economic model, children were expected only to assist family members. They used to be assigned roles according to their age and capability, but in the Industrial Revolution period, they were given difficult and dangerous tasks in the factory (Kirby, 2013). While they did not have sufficient knowledge about health and safety, they were assigned to operate dangerous machines. The employment was not fair, and there was no value of humanity. The industries were fully guided by the motive of profit in which the employers used to be considered as objects. To end such brutality employment law was passed in the 1830s that protected the basic rights of the employees (Mokyr, 2018).

Before the Industrial Revolution, there was mercantilism belief at the centre. And people used to think that there are finite resources in the world, which is insufficient to fulfil the market demand. People used to control resources and save for future uses. Also, every country used to focus on preserving the national resources. But the Industrial Revolution opposed such believe, and it advocated that there are infinite resources. And to increase national wealth resources should be used as much as possible instead of preserving it for the future. Then the use of resources dramatically increased across the world (King and Timmins, 2001). Later, liberalisation thoughts were spread across the world, and the philosophers like Adam Smith (1723-1790) argued that national wealth is necessary to get its public rid of poverty and starvation. This concept argues that the national wealth should be used by the public of that country (Gagnier, 2018). Further, based on the priorities, skills and desires, the wealth should be freely used; so that, the national wealth can be increased. Those kinds of philosophical thoughts set a strong foundation for American Declaration of Independent (1776).

Although the industrial revolution has a bundle of positive impacts in the society, some critics have noticed a few negative impacts as well. The condition of working-class people did not get any significant change which was one of the key problems of the Industrial Revolution. Although it advocated on quality of life to promote industry and increase national economy, life of working-class people remained miserable. Next, it remained unable to control population although some of the efforts were made; for instance, the industries used to pay low wages to discourage employees from increasing the number of children (Burgan, 2013). The authorities used to believe that if the employees have higher income, they can give birth more children and the population can be rapidly increased. The utilitarianism theory inspired that idea. And this theory argues that if an action has greater applicability in the society, such action has to be considered as successful. But this theory is no longer practical because it is impossible to evaluate everything based on utility (Schultz and Varouxakis, 2005). Also, it was blamed for creating a selfish and inhuman society. So, it was replaced by socialism theory which assumes that until and unless the economic gap is reduced, no equality and social harmony can be established. Also, this theory argues that working-class people should have control over the means of production, and there must be an equal distribution of share to everyone. In the response of utilitarianism theory, socialism theory was developed. It argued that all of the wealth should be nationalised and equally distributed to everyone. It assumed classless society that is free from corruption, dishonesty, and deception. In other words, it wants to create a utopian society that is compared to the heaven (Schumpeter, 1950). Socialism has become able to set a foundation to secure employment rights - job security, appropriate wages, holiday, break and proper working hours.

As the impact of the Industrial Revolution, the urban area became overcrowded, and it increased environmental pollution, crime, gender discrimination, and the economic gap between haves and haves not. According to Burgan (2013), poor people used to seek employment opportunity, but as they could not get a job, they used to involve in criminal activities. And to stop such crimes, police force was established. Also, people started to use the latest technology to prevent society from being affected by any crimes. Further, prisons were also built to keep the criminals out of society, where they used to get education and training to adjust back in the society (Hartwell, 2017). Online research publication of the British Museum (2017) also claims that during the Industrial Revolution period, rich people invested in the business, and poor people used to work for them. It made rich people richer, and the working-class people poorer (Schwab, 2017). The poor people started to send their children to the factories to earn some money to sustain their lives (Dixon, Gibbon and Gulliver, 2001). Also, Britain was experiencing political turmoil due to rapid industrialisation and urbanisation. And, quality education, human right, political right and social welfare became key concerns of the society. In 1807, Britain abolished the slave trade and began first step on securing human rights as the process of social reform (Allen, 2009).

1.3.5. Recent Trends of the Business

Technology accelerated at a faster pace than the expectation. Presently, the business has the following key attributes:

   A. Application of augmented intelligence (AI)
   B. Growing exercise of artificial intelligence
   C. Dramatic growth of automation
   D. Experience-based economy
   E. Rise of e-commerce
   F. Value created through bottom line
   G. Power shift from product to consumer

A. Application of Augmented Intelligence (AI)

Businesses, nowadays, are enormously relying on augmented intelligence (man + machine) for accuracy, effectiveness and efficiency of the workforce (Araya, 2018). Majority of the automobile companies are using AI software to fulfil the increased demand of the customers. It helps them to assemble more cars in short time duration that saves the organisation's operational cost and increases revenue and profitability. Due to low-cost production, the organisation can sell products/services at a lower price. It can be one of the key strategies to achieve competitive advantage, but it is difficult to sustain the competitive leverage because the competitors can easily adapt it. Airline companies are also using AI; for example, IBM's Watson software provides automatic information in case of passengers missed the connecting flight. So, the flight attendant can increase the effectiveness of its services through right action at the right time (Davenport, 2018). Also, marketing sectors can use AI. For example, to regulate dynamic pricing, rank products, analyse consumer behaviour and map the sales trend, Amazon Inc. has been using it. The AI software automatically produces information that underpins in making significant decision. In warehouse also, AI can be used to produce and distribute products. Automatic systems have been fixed in several warehouses to work automatically using machine, and the employees merely supervise the work of machine.

B. Growing Exercise of Artificial Intelligence

Artificial intelligence signifies to the machine intelligence, which is not natural (human and animal intelligence). Machine's human-like cognitive such as thinking, analysing, learning and problem-solving activities, are categorised under the AI. Nowadays, a computer can perform many actions related to storing and analysing information to resolve the problems. Besides, numbers of automobile companies including Waymo, GM and Ford have been trying to manufacture autonomous vehicles to independently function driver's activities like maintaining speed, stopping and analysing risk. Although the use of AI can be a great achievement, it can badly affect in job market. If the machine performs human cognitive power, there will be no or very little use of human resources. Also, there is a significant dispute in using AI in the business sector because it's reasoning, planning, learning and processing have several flaws (Jones, 2015).

C. Dramatic Growth of Automation

Automation is a process of performing activities with nominal human support. It partially replaces manual planning, implementation and control (Stanton, Salmon and Jenkins, 2009); so, through its support, an organisation can reduce its operational cost, time and effort. In the 21st century, several companies are using it to replace human resource and save their cost of research, production and delivery. For example, Budweiser has been using automation system in delivery. It has installed extra hardware and software to work as the driver. Such system thinks, communicates and makes decisions as human beings. Every day, it delivers products in the market using driverless technology which makes the business cost-effective and hassle-free. So, the organisation can sell its products at a lower price compared to the market price, which assists it to achieve sustainable competitive advantage (Culey, 2018). Similarly, Pizza Hut has been replacing its waiters by using robots. Besides, Walmart has also been using automation software to do accounting works (Foley et al., 2016). There are numbers of other organisations which have been using automation in their business operation. Along with the introduction of automation, traditional jobs have been significantly affected. But it helps business organisations easier to operate activities and fulfil customers needs and desires.

D. Experience Based Economy

In the 20th century, product quality and price were the major aspects to attract and retain customers. But nowadays, their preference has been changed. They want to be emotionally attached to the organisation either through a share or membership scheme (Baker, 2007). Of course, quality and price are essential factors, but as every organisation gives focus on quality and price, it cannot be enough to attract and retain the customers. In this situation, the customers expect something more that is "an emotional attachment." They want to be involved in the organisation's activities and find some ownership. At present, value can be created through different aspects including quality products, standard services and customers' involvement in the organisation's supply chain management process.

E. Rise of E-commerce

Along with commonly available Smartphone, computers and the internet services, online shopping got popularity in the new millennium. Giant e-commerce like Amazon was founded in 1994 by Jeff Bezos and eBay by Pierre Omidyar in 1995. These are two key international e-commerce companies which are based in the United

States of America. They have made shopping quite simple since the customers can search and order products online at any time and from elsewhere in the world (Laudon and Traver, 2015). They deliver the products at the customers' doors which saves customers' time and effort. Later on, several organisations have also entered into the e-commerce business. There is a significant role of internet banking system to develop e-commerce, which was introduced in the 1980s, but it got popularity in the 1990s (Cronin, 1998). Due to this system, e-commerce has become easier and more effective. Nowadays, physical stores do not only rely on their traditional mode of selling; along with physical stores, they are selling the products online as well. For example, supermarkets like Tesco, Sainsbury's, John Lewis, Marks and Spence, and Morrison started their businesses using traditional mode of sales, but later on, they have gone online. They know that customers are increasing in e-commerce; so, they quickly jumped online. At present, most of the physical stores have been adapting e-commerce as the complementary mode of sales.

F. Value Created through bottom Line

Nowadays, businesses are trying to create value through the bottom line. Although several customers do not want to donate any charity directly, they feel proud of the organisation that donates, which makes them loyal to the brand. For example, since Patagonia announced to give total revenue of Black Friday to the charity, it became able to increase the number of customers. As a result, it became able to sell over $10 million, which was five times more than the expectation (Middleton, 2018). Also, such contribution increased number of loyal customers. Many organisations are aware of customers' sentiment and to address it, they are contributing some portion of their profit to the charitable work. Supermarket chain like Sainsbury's has been working with Comic Relief as its corporate charity partner. It helped the organisation to raise over £30 million. Also, it has been regularly donating food to charitable organisations, including the Salvation Army and FareShare (Sainsbury's Website, 2016). Similarly, other organisations are also paying attention to helping needy people as a part of gaining customer loyalty and brand popularity.

G. Power Shift from Product to Consumer

In the business history, there is a substantial role of the industrial revolution because it brought a revolution in production sector by introducing machine. It brought change from agrarian and handicraft economy to machine manufacturing economy. Traditional means of production could not produce a large quantity of products as it would have to depend on the manual effort. So, there would be a low quantity of product, but the demand would be higher. Industrial revolution introduced new materials, machine and energy to fulfil increasing needs and demands in the market. Iron and steel were the basic material which were mined from the ground and processed later (McNeese, 2002). They were massively used to develop infrastructures including buildings, bridges and tower. Use of new resource of energy could also be another significant technological change in the industrial revolution. To run different machines, they started using steam, coal, electricity and petroleum resources. They started to use different types of energies which helped to produce more products and transport them from one place to another (Wolfe, 2015). If there were no energy, machine and technology, it would be impossible to produce mass product and distribute them across the world. But those machines were simple like the spinning jenny. On the foundation of those concepts of machine, organisations have become able to develop present advanced form of machines that fully shifted business from product centre to consumer centre.

In the industrial period, business organisations set a division of labour that helped to determine positions, wages, and terms and conditions of the employees. It brought industrial discipline and system that made organisations easy to operate their activities (Wolfe, 2015). Another important development was in the transportation sector. Steamship, steam locomotive, automobile and aeroplane were invented as the means of transportation at that age. Next significant change could be seen in the communication sector. At that phase, telegraph and radio were developed to communicate news and message in public (Dosi and Galambos, 2013). And the science was used as a part of business that systematically and scientifically explained the relationships of the business activities.

1.4. Types of Businesses

There are several types of businesses which can be studied by dividing into eight basic types:

A. Sole proprietorship
B. Partnership
C. Limited partnership
D. Corporation
E. Limited liability company
F. Non-profit organisation
G. Cooperative
H. Franchises

1.4.1. Sole Proprietorship

Sole proprietorship is the most popular type of business, which is easy to establish and operate because it has a single owner who has overall decision-making power. Different professionals including electrician, television repairer, garden cleaner and painter's small self-run businesses can be some of the examples of this type (Sitarz, 2011). Today, there are several web-based sole proprietorships, and they can be run from home. In this type of business, there is no difference between personal finance and business finance; the owner is fully responsible for every financial loss and legal issues (Bevans, 2006). For example, if the sole proprietorship has £50,000 loss, the owner has to fulfil the loss even from her/his private saving or property. Here, a business' liability or profitability mingles with owner's personal property which is one of its major drawbacks. But it has several merits like its registration process is simple and easy because it does not need to go through long legal procedure (Sitarz, 2011). Mostly businesses which are related to domestic products, small online businesses and low investment come under this type of business.

The key features of sole proprietorship are listed as follows:

- Single ownership
- Easier to establish
- Popular business type
- No legal and financial distinction between business owner and business
- Risk in personal property
- No registration hassle
- Suitable for online, domestic products/services and low investment businesses

1.4.2. Partnership

Partnership business type has two or more than two owners, where responsibilities and decision-making power are determined based on the business share that they own (Morse, 2010). It is highly suitable for the owner who is less experienced in a particular business sector because the partner's expertise helps him to learn new skills. Further, it shares potential financial and legal risks among the partners. This type is appropriate for the professional services including doctor, solicitor, accountant and others who can combine their skill and expertise to offer easier solutions for different problems.

This type of business requires to be registered with the company registering body, and it should require an official name. Since there are two or more than two owners, their share has to be stated while registering the business. The legal strength of the partner is determined based on the portion of the share. After registering, further licence might be required as the nature of the product or service that it deals. Also, it may require to register with internal revenue service (IRS) to pay tax on the profit. It can be highly suitable business type for an inexperienced business person because knowledge, experience, investment and business risk can be shared among the partners. Unlike a sole proprietorship, it separates business property and owner's personal property. It means to say that the owner is not liable to pay business liability from her/his private property (Douglas, 2008). For example, if business has £20,000 loss, by law, the owners will not be liable to pay the loss from their personal property or saving.

The key facts of this business type are listed as follow:

- Two or more than two owners
- Investment amount determines share and decision making power
- Need to be registered with the company registering body
- Demarcation between business property and owner's personal property
- Need to be registered with the IRS to pay tax
- Shared knowledge, experience, investment amount, workload and potential risks
- Extra paperwork
- Difficult in making decision

1.4.3. Limited Partnership

Limited partnership is a branch of partnership in which an investor invests, but she/he does not participate in day-to-day business operation. In this type of business, the investors can be divided into two types: general and limited. General investors have their business share; they actively participate in business activities, and they are liable for debts incurred. But limited investors only invest; they do not involve in business activities, and they are not liable for the debt incurred (Clifford and Warner, 2017). As a partnership business type, it should establish a business name and register with the state's company registering body as well with IRS (Meiners, Ringleb and Edwards, 2008).

The key facts of this business type are listed as follows:

- Less popular business type
- Suitable for passive investors
- Two types of investors: general and limited (general investor - involves in day-to-day management and liable for debt, limited investor - no involvement in day-to-day management and not liable for debt)
- Need to give business name, and register with state's company registering body and with IRS
- Suitable for multiple partners
- More paperwork

1.4.4. Corporation

Corporation is an independent organisation which can have multiple shareholders who collect capital and have decision making power. It pays business tax on the profit and dividend to the shareholders who have to pay personal income tax on it. In this regard, there will be a double tax (business and personal) on the profit of the corporation. This kind of business can have multiple employees, and it can be larger. It has to be registered with the state business registering body and with IRS. Further, it may require an appropriate licence as per the nature of products that it deals with (Drucker, 2009).

The key facts of this business type are listed as follows:

- Independent business
- Collects capital from shareholders
- Multiple employees
- Double tax on profit (business and personal level)
- Register with state business registering body and with IRS

1.4.5. Limited Liability Company

Limited liability company (LLC) is a new type of business that shares attributes from sole proprietorship and corporation. So, it can be understood as the blend of sole proprietorship and corporation (Cody, Hopkins and Perlman, 2007). It can have many owners who can be listed as the managing members, and they can be involved in day to day business activities. It does not need to pay tax as a separate business which implies that its profit or loss can be calculated and taxed as personal income. Also, its owners are not personally liable for the business decision, and it does not require extensive paperwork.

The key facts of this business type are listed as follows:

- Blend of sole proprietorship and corporation
- Multiple owners
- No business tax
- Owners' involvement in day to day operation
- Owners are not personally liable for business decision
- Easier to establish (less paperwork)

1.4.6. Non-profit Organisation

Non-profit organisations have key involvement in social welfare activities, including social awareness, social education, health care, food collection for needy people and many more. Its members contribute their time and effort for others' welfare instead of their benefits. All capital earned by this type of organisation is spent to cover its expenses and fulfil the organisation's goals (Drucker, 2012). Here, the business owner or the members do not earn any profit; rather, they spent their time, effort and money to fulfil the objectives. As the purpose of this organisation is related to social welfare, its earning will be tax-free (Drucker, 2012). The donor also need not to pay tax on the earning amount that she/he donates. For instance, if Sam has a £10,000 tax payable amount, he has to pay 20% (£2,000) personal tax. But if he is going to donate £5,000 to a charity organisation, he should not pay tax of this amount - he has to pay tax on the remaining £5,000 which will be only £1,000.

The key facts of this type business are listed as follows:

- No profit-earning operation
- Social welfare motto
- Tax-free earnings
- Total earnings are spent to cover the organisation's expenses
- Less paperwork and easy to register

1.4.7. Co-operative

Co-operative is one of the important business types which is run by its members who are called cooperative members. The co-operative members can only buy its share, and they have decision making power of the organisation. Its major propose is to increase members' share value. This type of organisation must have to create its members and a board of director. Like other organisations, it has to be registered with the state's company registering body after it has created members and board of directors. Then, it has to be registered with IRS for tax purpose (Patmore and Balnave, 2018).

The key facts of this business type are listed as follows:

- Need to create membership
- Benefits to its members
- Register with the state's company registering body and IRS
- Members have decision making power

1.4.8. Franchises

Franchises are understood as the licensing agreements that allows an individual or group to operate business activities under the particular brand name and system. In other words, the franchisor grants a licence to the franchisee and that licence entitles franchisees to own and operate business organisation under franchisor's brand name, system and model (Mendelsohn, 2005). The franchisee receives training, human resource management support, technical supports and other necessary supports from franchisor. In return, the franchisee pays certain royalty to the franchisor, which is determined based on annual turnover. The franchise agreement determines the terms and conditions. Normally, the contract term period can be five years and renewable (Barkoff and Selden, 2008).

Lots of international organisations, including McDonald's, Coca Cola, and Subway, are using franchise growth and development model. Due to the franchise, customers get the same ambience and same major products in McDonald's across the world. Although it is a franchise, it should be registered with the company registering body of the state, and it has to pay tax as a separate entity. The franchisee has control over the business, but in case of other issues like marketing, products/services development, quality, standard and models, the franchisor has a direct control. The franchisee has the flexibility to make some changes without affecting the core value of the organisation. It means to say that it cannot change major product and ambience, but minor changes can be made as per required (Barkoff and Selden, 2008).

The key facts of this business type are listed as follows:

- Agreement between franchisor and franchisee
- Entitle to operate business under franchisor's brand name, system and model
- Easier to run the business
- Technical and HRM support from franchisor
- Franchisee pays royalty to franchisor
- Register with state's company registering body
- Much more paperwork
- Renewable licence agreement

1.5. Public and Private Companies

By ownership, companies can be either public or private. Public company is a bigger business organisation which should be registered with company house or state's company registering body. It develops constitutions or code of conducts that govern its shareholders and assist in operating the business activities (Bruno and Ruggiero, 2011). To be a company, it has to fulfil some criteria set by state. For example, in the United Kingdom, it must be registered with Companies House. Also, it must have a minimum £50,000 allocated share capital with at least 25% fully paid. And it must have certificate for commencement of trading, which is issued by the Companies House (Hannigan, 2012).

Public company is an independent legal entity; thereby, it is liable to pay business tax on profit. The shareholders again have to pay personal tax on the dividend. It means to say that it will have twice taxed on the profit. As it is an independent body, the shareholder is not liable to pay its liability from the personal fund (Hannigan, 2012). But, it can sell its share freely in public, and its shares can be listed on a stock exchange. By selling the shares, it can generate the required capital to grow and develop further or pay back the loan. By law, the public company requires at least two directors. It cannot accept any ongoing work as the portion of share, which means to say that without accomplishing work, it cannot be added in the share. The companies cannot buy their share out of their capital. By law, they have to file the annual account within nine months. Also, they must have to appoint a qualified secretary. And they must have to hold an annual general meeting by law (Hannigan, 2012).

The key facts of the public company are listed as follows:

- Exist as a separate business entity
- Can be owned by local or central government
- Must appoint at least two directors and one secretary
- Must be registered with the state's company registering body
- Can issue shares to the general public and raise capital

- Must submit an annual report (within nine months)
- Cannot buy its shares out of its capital
- Much paperwork to allocate shares
- Must hold least a general meeting in a year

Private limited companies (PVT LTD) are also independent business entity in which shareholders' liabilities are limited to the value of share. As a private company, it cannot offer shares to the public, unlike the public companies. Different states and nations have different rules and regulations that guide how to form and operate a PVT LTD (Brough, 2005). For example, in the United States, it should be incorporated with the state's company registering body. And it must have minimum one director, who should be the primary shareholder. If there are multiple shareholders, they can be considered as the directors (Levy, 2013). Unlike the public company, it does not have any compulsion to appoint a company secretary. They have to file annual accounts within six months. At the end of every financial year, it has to submit an annual return to the company registering body. Also, by law, they are not obliged to hold an annual general meeting. If a private company wants to transform into a public company, it can be easily upgraded, but it requires much paperwork. If an organisation has growth opportunities, switching into a public company can be beneficial. Otherwise, transforming into a public company may increase unnecessary cost, consume much time, and increase legal complications (Brough, 2005).

The key facts of the private company are listed as follows:

- Separate business entity than the owner's personal property
- Must appoint a director
- Must register with the state's company registering body
- Cannot issue share to the public to raise capital
- Must submit annual report
- Can easily upgrade into a public company
- Less paperwork
- No compulsion for holding general meeting(s)

1.6. Difference between Public Companies and Public Sectors

Sometimes people might be in confuse about public companies and public sectors, and they consider both are synonymous to each other. But they are quite different because public companies are those businesses which are owned by individuals (shareholders). If that company is a corporation, the stock can be traded in a stock exchange. But public-sector indicates to the government-owned or controlled organisations in which the state or central government holds 51% or more share. It is imperative to say that the major purpose of the public sector is to provide essential public service to the community by employing the state's resources. The government can fund some of the corporations, but it does not have control over them. In the UK, BBC and Royal Mail are the public companies in which the government provides grants. Some of the companies charge for the products or services, but the income is used to run the companies' day to day activities (Floyd, 2006).

CHAPTER 2

Beginning a Business - Key Procedures

2.1. Market Research

An organisation's success or failure depends upon the brand image in the market. As the business satisfies target customers, it can be successful in achieving competitive advantage. The market is perpetually changing due to growing expectations of the customers and harsh competitive market environment. So, to sustain in the market, every business organisation needs to bring some changes and those changes can be in any sector including product, service, strategy and business model.

Market research helps an organisation to identify customers' needs and desires. Jackson and Shaw (2008) say, "Market research refers to the part of the marketing function concerned with developing insights into customers' needs, wants and preferences." It tries to clarify that it is an activity of collecting market insight to develop suitable business strategies and fulfil the organisation's strategic objectives. Marketing executives use market information for exploring opportunities, developing suitable marketing actions, controlling marketing performance and evaluating marketing actions (Strydom, 2005). A business can have several choices on different sectors including place, product, target customer, price, process, and many more. If the organisation becomes able to select the most suitable option(s), it contributes to fulfil business objectives; otherwise, it faces several obstacles. Here, the market research plays a crucial role to select the most suitable option. It provides the depth insights into the overall market situation in which it is going to operate its business activities.

2.1.1. Data

Booksmart (2014) says that data are "the raw facts", but as they are processed, they are understood as information. There is a crucial role of data to accomplish research since, without data, the conclusion cannot be justifiable, reliable and generalisable. It means to say that the data is the backbone of the research; thereby, the most suitable and fair data have to be collected. Kothari (2009) says that by collection, there are two types of data: primary and secondary.

2.1.1.1. Primary Data and its Collection Methods

Primary data is fresh information which is collected by the researcher directly visiting the field. The researcher visits or contacts sample respondents and collects necessary information. These data can be up to date and more relevant but to collect such data, it will cost more time, money and effort. There are numbers of primary data collection instruments like interview, focus group, questionnaire, observation, case study and scientific experiment.

A. Interview

Interview is one of the key data collection instruments in which the interviewer asks questions to the interviewee who answers as per her/his knowledge and experience (Kothari, 2009). It can be either a face to face or telephone interview. This instrument is applicable to collect subjective information using open-ended questions (Pulliam and Stawarski, 2008). It is easy to formulate question and collect intensive information. But it has some limitations such as it cannot include a wider range of sample respondent. Also, it is a time-consuming data collection instrument. Further, the data can be affected by the prejudice of the researchers, and it can be costly as well (Source: Kothari, 2009).

By structure, it can be divided into three types: structured, semi-structured and unstructured. Structured interview is fully pre-planned in which the interviewer does not have any flexibility to amend it. She/he has to ask the pre-planned questions and record the answers (Kothari, 2009). It puts the researcher off from collecting deeper and clearer answer. Just opposite to structured interview, unstructured interview has nothing pre-planned; thereby, interviewer's role is quite crucial. The quality and relevance of the data fully depends upon the skills and expertise of the researcher. Since it is not pre-planned, sometimes, it can collect the data that is not relevant to the particular research (Bailey, 2008). And semi-structured interview combines the merits of both types of interviews (Structured and Unstructured). Here, everything is pre-planned that ensures the collected data are relevant to the research. Also, it provides flexibility to the interviewer to do cross-questions and collect deeper and clearer information (Kothari, 2009).

B. Focus Group

Focus group refers to a group of 6-12 people to whom the researcher gives a particular topic to discuss in the natural environment. The respondents express their feelings, emotions and experiences spontaneously on the topic. Henderson (2009) says that a focus group is, basically, a qualitative data collection instrument in which the participants are asked about their perceptions, attitudes or beliefs towards certain product, service, concept, adverting, idea or packaging. In the focus group, the researcher does not interfere or influence the members of the group. In the given subject matter, the sample participants express their views from different angles and the researcher notes down the important points. According to Kothari (2009), there are different types of focus groups like two-way focus group, dual moderate focus group, duelling moderate focus group, respondent moderate focus group, client participant focus group, mini focus group, teleconference focus group and online focus group.

Focus group is suitable to collect valuable insights by using a detailed discussion based on idea, memory and experience. It is cost-effective, easier and quicker data collection instrument in which the respondents can discuss openly and freely in unstructured design (Henderson, 2009). But the researcher does not have control over the group, and sometimes the discussion can be out of track (Kothari, 2009). Also, to collect the most relevant information, the participants must be energetic, enthusiastic and motivated. And if the respondents do not have a common language, it may require translator(s) (Kothari, 2009).

C. Questionnaire

According to Kothari (2009), a questionnaire is a set of questions that is prepared to gather information from the sample respondents. Mostly, it is designed to collect quantitative information, but it does not mean that it cannot be used to collect qualitative information. To collect quantitative information, it includes close-ended questions like multiple choice or yes/no. Although developing close-ended questions is a complex job, answering can be easier and quicker. Also, it is a cost-effective means of primary data collection instrument that covers a wider range of participants from any corner of the world. Questionnaires can be posted or emailed to the respondents if they are located far away (Phillips and Stawarski, 2016). But if they are in closer distance, the researcher can visit them and ask to fill the questionnaire. While returning the questionnaire, the respondents use the same means by which they have received the questionnaire. According to Kothari (2009), it easily reaches to the busy people, and further, they can fill it in their free time. It is not affected by the researcher's prejudice since she/he cannot influence the respondents while collecting data. But according to Saunders, Lewis, and Thornhill (2009), this method has a low response rate if it is emailed or posted, and the postal method might be time-consuming as well. Similarly, they say that the questionnaire is not applicable to collect subjective information.

D. Observation

According to Bryman and Bell (2015), observation is "a method where the researcher provides an explicitly formulated rules for the observation and recording of behaviour." It helps to collect reliable data because, in it, the researcher can use various senses to collect the data. But, it is a time-consuming, costly and difficult data collection instrument that demands trained and skilful researcher.

E. Case Study

Case study is one of the key data collection instruments, which excels at bringing an understanding of a complex issue (Yin, 2013). It adds experience or knowledge on the previous researches. Gagnon (2010) argues that although it is limited to few cases, it goes depth in the issue. Mostly, it can be applied in secondary research, particularly in the qualitative research, to conduct a systematic review over the previous researches.

F. Scientific Experiment

Scientific experiment data collection instrument refers to collecting objective information using human senses. And the collected information are tested in the scientific laboratory or real-life situation (Kothari, 2009). It is applicable to experiment the relationships between dependent and independent variables to test the hypothesis. According to Wilson (2010), it is mostly used to investigate the research issues related to natural science and psychology. But it is time consuming, costly and difficult data collection instrument.

2.1.1.2. Secondary Data Collection

Secondary data are already collected information by the previous researchers. They are recorded in research articles, journals, books, videos or newspapers; so, they can be collected from the library or internet sources (Bryman, 2015). As they can be easily gathered by sitting on the desk, sometimes, they are called as the "desk data."

A researcher does not need to spend much time, money and effort to collect these types of data (Kothari, 2009). But there might be thousands of information, and selecting the most suitable might be a quite challenging job. Similarly, they may not be up-to-date; thereby, most of the data can be irrelevant in the current situation. If the data are not relevant and up-to-date, the conclusion cannot be reliable, which may mislead activities of business organisations (Saunders, Lewis and Thornhill, 2009). In this regard, while collecting the secondary information, one must be practical and focus on the research objectives (Bryman and Bell, 2015). While collecting secondary data, the researcher has to narrow down the research topic because there might be lots of related secondary information. If the area is too wide, the researcher can be deviated from the actual subject matter, and it becomes difficult in fulfilling the research objectives (Kothari, 2009).

While conducting market research, the researcher may require different types of data, for example, information about the target market, economic situation, alternative products, frequency of uses and many more. The collected data are the raw information which should be analysed to get their underlying meaning. And based on research conclusion, business organisations make their decisions (Kothari, 2009). A well-planned research helps to determine key business decisions about product, price, place, promotion, people, physical evidence and process based on the market research.

2.2. Data Analysis Techniques

Data analysis is a process of systematic and scientific evaluation of the collected information. It processes information, identifies trend and derives meaningful conclusion (Sekaran and Bougie, 2016). There are various data analysis techniques, but a researcher has to select the most suitable one. If the selected data analysis technique is wrong, the research cannot come to the valid conclusion. Based on data, it divides into three types: qualitative, quantitative and mixed.

2.2.1. Qualitative Data Analysis Techniques

Qualitative data analysis technique is used to analyse subjective or qualitative data. It is mainly used to understand social phenomenon in a natural setting through the means of participants' knowledge, view and experience (Mason, 2017). There are different types of qualitative analysis techniques:

1. Content analysis
2. Narrative analysis
3. Discourse analysis
4. Framework analysis
5. Grounded theory
6. Case study
7. Phenomenological technique
8. Ethnography

2.2.1.1. Content Analysis

Content analysis is the process of collecting, tabulating and summarising verbal or behavioural information. The data can be either described or interpreted to derive a valid conclusion. This type of analysis focuses on getting the meaning of the particular content either through descriptive or interpretative method (Neuendorf, 2016). Descriptive content analysis merely describes data - it answers the question "what is the data", but the interpretative data analysis explains "what the data mean." Descriptive analysis merely tries to understand the content, but interpretative analysis interprets information using the most suitable theory or model (Kothari, 2009). If the data are interpreted without using any theory or model, the interpretation can be biased, and that cannot solve the research problem. In the research, both levels of analysis can be used for an effective analysis. If the data are clearly defined and interpreted, it will be easy to get the underlying meaning.

2.2.1.2. Narrative Analysis

Narrative denotes to a story or experience of the sample respondent. According to Kothari (2009), interview and observation might have some narratives which should be identified, sorted out and presented legibly by the researcher. Different respondents may present their stories in their styles and in different contexts which can be difficult to understand. In this regard, the researcher has to reformulate stories and present a story that should cover every important aspect of the stories. In narrative analysis, the researcher notes down the key aspects to remind them in the analysis process. There might be numbers of insignificant information which should be ignored and reformulated to make it as subtle and short as possible. This type of data analysis technique is suitable to report incident or experience.

2.2.1.3. Discourse Analysis

Discourse analysis evaluates the nature of everyday occurring communication (verbal) and any written texts (non-verbal). It is highly suitable to analyse linguistic subject matter as it emphasises on the way language is being used to fulfil everyday social life (Taylor, 2013). This analysis argues that there might be different expressions and their meanings can be associated with particular context. Body language, expression, symbol, metaphor, reference, and context are important indicators of discourse analysis as they help to clarify the meaning (Taylor, 2013). If a researcher ignores them, factual meaning can appear in distorted form, and such meaning cannot solve the problem. In the market research, sometimes, this analysis can be applied to understand consumer behaviour. If the target consumers participate in a focus group, this analysis can be applied to understand the meaning of their conversation on a given topic. As the meaning or important points are clearly understood, they can be noted down, and further analysis like interpretation can be carried out if required.

2.2.1.4. Framework Analysis

Framework analysis is one of the popular qualitative data analysis models, which has been using in management research to resolve research problem since 1980s (Ritchie and Lewis, 2003). It emphases on comparing and contrasting data to find the conclusion. It provides seven steps of data analysis process that makes analysis effective and efficient. In other words, it is a structured analysis process that fully guides a researcher step by step from beginning to ending. Although it is an effective analysis method, it has some limitations as it cannot accommodate highly heterogeneous data, and it is not that much easy to apply in practice. It is useful to conduct a thematic analysis of subjective data, especially that are collected from semi-structured interview data collection instrument (Gale and et al., 2013). There are different stages of this model:

Stage 1: Transcription

The data collected from the interview can be in the audio form, which should be transcribed into the written form for its analysis. Audio data is difficult to code, describe, interpret; thereby, it must be transcribed. But while transcribing, original meaning or sense of the data should not be distorted. And more space or line gap in transcription page makes the coding process easier (Ritchie and Lewis, 2003).

Stage 2: Internalisation of Interview

In this stage, the researcher has to be familiar with interview (by listening the audio recording and reading the transcribed data), which helps her/him to understand information. And while understanding the data, the researcher might have some comments, thoughts or feelings which have to be noted on the margin of the transcription (Gubrium et al., 2012).

Stage 3: Coding

In the third stage, the researcher carefully reads every single line word by word and gives codes for each important line. At least two researchers have to code the first few transcribes independently; so, the major aspects of the transcribed document cannot be missed. And the code should be, later on, compared and contrasted with the rest of the transcribes (Adu, 2019).

Stage 4: Developing a Common Framework

Due to the involvement of different researchers, there might be variations in coding. But the researchers have to work together and find the common framework by reducing such variations. The codes can be grouped into different categories and developed a tree diagram that helps to categorise the rest of the transcribes. In the developed category, new code can be included if it is found later on (Adu, 2019). It means to say that, the framework cannot be final until the last transcribe is coded and grouped.

Stage 5: Applying the Framework

Each code is assigned a particular number or abbreviation that helps to identify the code easily. The codes and categories are, at this state, systematically catalogued or indexed. To systematically store, it can be accomplished manually. According to Adu (2019), if Computer Assisted Qualitative Data Analysis Software (CAQDAS) is available, the data can be easily stored and retrieved as needed. But this software cannot be used to analyse the data.

Stage 6: Generating Framework Matrix

In this stage, the data should be presented in a matrix in which the researcher has to focus on squeezing the data in short form without distorting the original meaning. To generate matrix, CAQDAS or N-Vivo software can be applicable. This matrix summarises the key information of the entire data (Bazeley and Jackson, 2013).

Stage 7: Data Interpretation

Based on the framework matrix, the researcher presents an interpretation of the collected information. She/he can use any note that she/he had written in different stages of the framework analysis. According to Bazeley and Jackson (2013), this method expects multiple researchers who discuss important notes (that they have made) and the framework matrix (that they have derived). Then they come up with a common conclusion to resolve the research problem.

2.2.1.5. Grounded Theory

Grounded theory collects qualitative data and explains them based on the particular theory. It examines whether the collected data fit under a particular theory or not. Today, its area has been extended to set ground for a new theory as well. In it, the researcher reviews the data; finds concept, and codes them. Then, she/he categorises the codes and explains to discover an emerging pattern of data, which helps to develop a new theory. And such theory can be later applied to assess similar type of research issues (Bazeley and Jackson, 2013). This data analysis method begins with particular information and comes to the general conclusion, which means to say that it uses inductive approach. As mentioned earlier, it collects qualitative data, reviews, codes and categorises them. These categories are interpreted from different angles to determine reliable and generalisable theory or concept.

2.2.1.6. Case Study

Case study is an important qualitative data analysis technique which is suitable to explain an event or organisation. As it includes a few cases, it can collect extensive and deeper level of data. Mostly, it is used to explore complicated issue through the means of deeper analysis. As per the nature of the case, it can be explanatory, exploratory or descriptive research. Also, it can use different types of data collection instruments to collect relevant data. According to Harrison et al. (2017) case study research technique has been "capable of providing comprehensive, in-depth understanding of a diverse range of issues across several disciplines." It collects data from particular cases and develops a generalisable concept which means to say that it uses inductive reasoning approach. Usually, it uses qualitative data, but if necessary, it can also use quantitative data.

2.2.1.7. Phenomenological Technique

Phenomenological data analysis technique describes information based on a particular event or activity. It collects qualitative information and describes them to clarify the phenomenon. The data can be collected through different sources including observation, interview and library (Saunders, Lewis and Thornhil, 2009). Usually, the conclusion is derived based on themes formulated from interview; thereby, it requires more data from a higher number of interviewees. While evaluating the data, the researcher evaluates various aspects such as language, emotion, belief, feeling and attitude that helps to find research themes. It believes that the object is the essence and beyond it, meaning cannot be generated (Moustakas, 1994); so, it emphasises on the event or activity. It organises, codes and categories the information to develop theme(s). While evaluating it does not depend on any assumption, theory and model. It believes that the event cannot be replaced or understood going beyond the phenomenon; thereby, the information is objectively described that helps to derive objective conclusion. It uses inductive reasoning approach as it generates themes through information of the particular event or activity.

2.2.1.8. Ethnography

Ethnography research explores the underlying problems of the particular tribe or ethnic group and resolves them. Most of the sociological and anthropological researches use this type of data analysis method. While using this research method, the researcher may require to stay together with the particular tribe in which she/he is going to conduct a research. Then, she/he closely observes activities of that tribe, and she/he can interview with the member(s) of the tribe (Saunders, Lewis and Thornhil, 2009). As there is observation, it has less possibility of misunderstanding the information. The collected information should be explained based on the context of the particular tribe rather than using any theory or model.

2.2.2. Quantitative Data Analysis Techniques

Quantitative data analysis techniques make a rational and valid judgement over objective information. It explores relationships between variables by calculating frequencies and differences. It objectively tests the hypothesis based on the relationship and makes an objective decision. And the relationship can be examined through computer software programmes like SPSS and Excel. There are different types of quantitative research techniques which are listed below:

1. Descriptive research
2. Observational method
3. Case study
4. Survey method
5. Correlation research
6. Experimental research

2.2.2.1. Descriptive Research

Descriptive research logically and systematically describes key attributes of the information. This type of research gives more emphasis on "what" question rather than "why." Similarly, neither it makes any prediction nor finds the cause and effect of the information; it only describes to make information easier to understand. By nature, it is more applicable for qualitative research; thereby, it is not that much popular in quantitative research. There are three different types of descriptive research as observation, case study and survey (Mitchell and Jolley, 2009).

2.2.2.2. Observational Method

Observation method closely observes an object or event to identify the key characteristics. Such characteristics can be described to make them easier to understand. It has two types: naturalistic observation and laboratory observation (McBurney and White, 2009).

In the naturalistic observation, the researcher participates with participants in natural environment and obtains factual information (McBurney and White, 2009). This type of observation can collect respondents' feelings, emotions and pathos. And those data better represent research issue; so, the findings can be more accurate, useful and reliable.

But laboratory observation gives more focus on laboratory research. This type of observation has strong control over information; thereby, it can be more meaningful. Also, it is less time consuming and more cost-effective observation compared to naturalist observation. However, it cannot collect as actual information as naturalistic observation. (McBurney and White, 2009.

2.2.2.3. Case Study

Case study is another type of qualitative research that involves an in-depth study of the particular event, issue, organisation or individual. It is not used to find out cause and effect; rather, it is used to make an accurate prediction (Saunders, Lewis and Thornhil, 2009). From different cases, a researcher collects quantitative data which are described to find out the underlying trend in the overall data. For a valid and reliable conclusion, such description should be bias-less and based on facts.

2.2.2.4. Survey Method

Survey research method collects information either through interview or questionnaire. The researcher merely describes such information; she/he does not seek any relationship between the variables (Kothari,

2009). It is applicable for the quantitative research which does not have complicated research issue. It collects quantitative data and describes them to get the conclusion. If the research issue is complicated, it requires adapting qualitative research method.

2.2.2.5. Correlation Research

Unlike descriptive research, correlation research measures two variables and finds out their relationships. It tries to answer "how" question by testing data in statistic software or scientific laboratory. As the relationship is tested in software or laboratory, it obtains objective relationship. It is an objective research method in which the researcher's prejudice does not have any room to influence data analysis process. So, it can derive a valid, reliable and generalisable conclusion (McBurney and White, 2009). It uses a correlation coefficient test to find the relationship between two variables where the measurement can be in between -1 and +1. Here, close to +1 shows a positive relationship and close to -1 shows a negative relationship; close to zero shows neutral or no-relationship. Sometimes, there might be more than two variables which cannot be tested by using correlation as this method is only suitable for two variables. A regression analysis test can be used to test the relationship between multiple variables, whereas the measurement range and result types can be the same as mentioned in the correlation coefficient.

2.2.2.6. Experimental Research

Experimental research manipulates groups/levels of independent variables and measures the outcome. It is a suitable technique to assess the cause and effect. Here, the independent variables are treated differently, and the impacts are compared with dependent variables. According to Kothari (2009), this kind of research can be carried out in a real-life situation as well as the laboratory test. There are two key experimental research designs: true experiment and quasi-experiment. Major purpose of both types of research can be to find the cause of particular effect or problem. In both types of research, the participants should be experimented under some treatments or conditions, and the outcomes of each group is minutely measured.

True experimental research randomly assigns participants in the treatment or the control groups. According to Cash, Stankovic and Storga (2016) in both groups, the same treatment is applied; thereby, it is very easy for the researcher to control the treatment. Due to the strong control, it has less chance to have several hypothesis which makes the research easier to conclude in less time, effort and money.

Quasi-experimental research does not randomly assign the population as the research group. The researcher has weak control in this test, which arouses a question regarding its validity of the findings. While analysing the data through this research method, firstly, the variables should be identified (dependent and independent variables). Here, the independent variable is marked as x-variable, which is manipulated as required to affect the dependent variable (y-variable). X-variables are divided into several groups, and different interventions will be applied for different groups. The predicted outcome is the y-variable which means to say that the effects of treatment on the x-variable groups are expected to see similar to the effects on y-variables. Cash, Stankovic and Storga (2016) say that researcher's personal choice is key to determine factor to select samples, treatment and grouping. There is no clear rule or criteria for selection; so, the researcher can make decision based on cost, feasibility, time, and other aspects. In this regard, there is a question about internal validity.

2.2.3. Mixed Data Analysis Techniques

As the research issue is much complicated, it may require both qualitative and quantitative types of data to which a mixed data analysis technique is required. This technique can use both qualitative and quantitative technique as per required. In qualitative research, only qualitative data analysis technique is used, and in quantitative research, only quantitative data analysis technique is applied. But in the mixed research, both types of data analysis techniques can be applied. It helps the researcher to conduct a depth analysis of different issues and find out cause and effect relationship.

2.3. Understanding Consumer Behaviour

An individual who consumes the product or uses the service is a consumer and her/his all activities related to purchases are the consumer behaviours. Blackwell, Miniard and Engel (2006) say that consumer behaviour is the total activities of a consumer related to obtaining, consuming and disposing the product and service. Similarly, Angel, Kollat and Blackwell (1968) also define consumer behaviour as the total buying activities from obtaining to disposing the products.

To retain the customers, an organisation has to address their needs and desires, but until and unless an organisation does not understand the consumer behaviour, it cannot identify those needs and desires. According to Blackwell, Miniard and Engel (2006), consumer behaviour is not limited within certain area. Whether we surf the restaurant menu or we see the advertising or we enter into the retail, consumer behaviour can be activated. However, all of the behaviours are guided by the needs and satisfaction. That is the reason, by acknowledging the consumer behaviour, an organisation can provide the most suitable products and services to attract, satisfy and retain the customers (Blackwell, Miniard and Engel, 2006). Jethwaney and Jain (2007) highlight some of the benefits of understanding consumer behaviour:

- It helps to analyse the market condition
- It contributes to determine appropriate target segment
- It supports to set the strategic objectives
- It underpins to increase performance level

Based on trait, there are four types of consumer behaviour: innovativeness, materialism, self-consciousness and need for cognition (Russell, 1984).

Innovative consumer behaviour wants to experiment with novel products and services. But the materialism consumer behaviour enjoys with material goods; so that, such type of consumers buy materials/products like computer, mobile and TV. But the self-conscious consumer behaviour is interested in buying products and services that could address reasonable needs and desires. And the cognition consumer behaviour buys the products and services to increase the level of knowledge and understanding in different sectors (Belk, 1984).

2.3.1. Influence in Consumer Behaviour

There are several factors including consumer need, economic situation, culture, tradition, product and service that determine consumer behaviour. Consumer behaviour can be understood differently, based on influencing factors. For example, an economic element defines consumer behaviour based on money and time, whereas cultural element defines it as the process of fulfilling social and personal needs (Perreault and McCarthy, 2006). Needs meet the essential function of human life, and they are the underlying forces of motivation (Dummies, 2009). Although some people consider need and want as synonymous terms, they are different to each other. Needs are primary desires which are related to the basic function of the natural body, but wants are optional or additional that the people learn during the living. For example, fulfilling hunger is the basic need, but what especially people prefer to eat might be the want. Solomon (2004) divides needs into four types: biogenic, psychogenic, utilitarian and hedonic. He says that biogenic needs are associated with necessities including air, water, and food, but the psychogenic needs are associated with power, love, status and many more. Utilitarian is the third need that is determined by the purpose, and they are tangible and objective, whereas hedonic needs are experimental and highly subjective.

Similarly, Perrearult and McCarthy (2006) also categorise needs into different four parts as physiological, safety, social and personal. Perrearult and McCarthy (2006) say that physiological needs are associated with biological necessities which could be fulfilled by food, drink, rest and sex. Protection and physical well beings are related to safety need. Personal needs are related to personal fun and enjoyment. And social needs concern with friendship, status, love and esteem.

Maslow's (1970) hierarchical need theory is renowned for describing needs. According to Maslow (1970), there are five types of needs: physiological, safety, belongingness, esteem and self-actualisation, which are in the hierarchical order where the higher need is fulfilled only after the fulfilling the lower needs (figure 2).

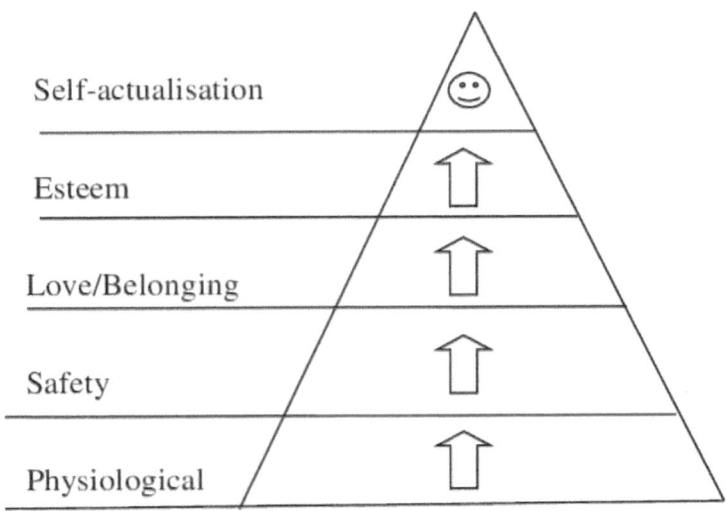

Figure 2: Maslow's hierarchy need

According to Maslow (1970), physiological needs are fulfilled by food, water, air and others. Safety needs are related to security, shelter and protection, whereas love or belonging is related to feeling of love and care. Esteem or ego is fulfilled by respect, prestige and status. And self-actualisation is relevant to self-fulfilment, and enriching experiences to be dominant.

2.3.2. Consumer Buying Behaviour Process

Although consumer buying behaviours are affected by various internal and external factors, it follows a specific process. Consumer buying behaviour comes under a precise and systematic process that is regarded "the decision making processes and acts of individuals involved in buying and using products or services (Dib et al., 2001)." Various scholars have introduced different types, but Ferrell and Hartline's (2008), five processes are widely used in the market. They are problem/need recognition, information search, evaluation of different purchase options, purchase decision, and post-purchase behaviour (see in figure 3).

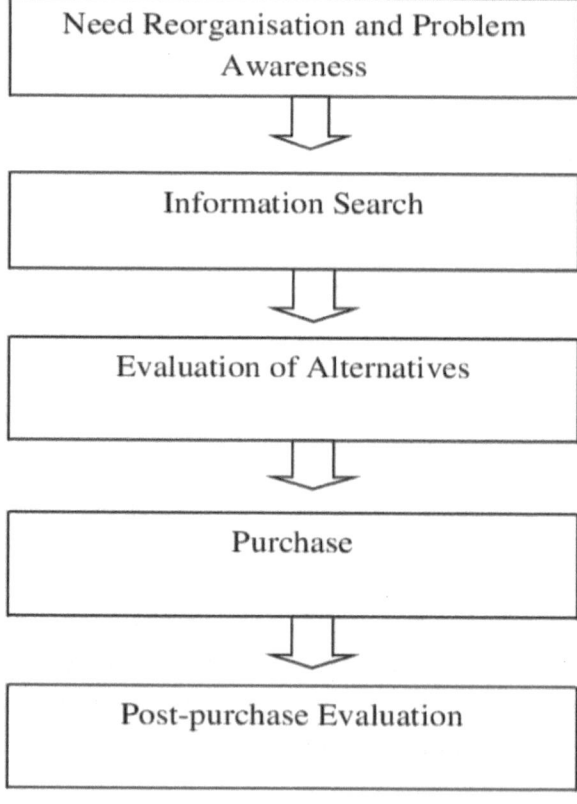

Figure 3: Consumer buying behaviour process

A. Problem/Need Recognition

Need recognition is the first step of consumer buying behaviour process. In this stage, the consumers feel something lacking as they identify the difference between their idea and real situation. Then, it arouses an interest to have something that could fulfil the an actual necessity.

B. Information Search

As the consumers determine to accomplish lacking, they start to collect information about the potential products and services that could satisfy their need. To search the data, they recall the knowledge and experience, consult with the family members, friends, relatives, and review the advertisements, feedback and websites.

C. Evaluation of Different Purchase Options

In the market, there might be various options/substitutions; different brands are competing with similar products and services. So, the consumers should evaluate the alternatives based on attributes like price, quality and quantity that helps them to find the best option.

D. Purchase Decision

When the consumers assess the available options, they come to purchase decision. It is a crucial stage since the consumers have to decide which product or service will be the most suitable for them. And they use it to fulfil their needs and desires.

E. Post-purchase Behaviour/Evaluation

Finally, based on the product and service that they used, they build an attitude about the brand or organisation. If their needs are fulfilled, they can be loyal, and they recommend it to the family members, relatives and friends. But if they are not satisfied, they do not become loyal to the brand, and they provide negative feedback to others.

2.4. Market Segmentation and Targeting

Market is an umbrella term that accommodates several types of consumers. An organisation may not be able to fulfil every consumer's need; thereby, market segmentation and targeting are necessary. If a restaurant sells Indian cuisine that only meets the needs of Indian food-loving customers but not the needs of Chinese or other food-loving customers; so that, for that restaurant, only Indian food-loving customers might be the principal target segment.

In marketing, segmentation and targeting are understood as the complementary terms to each other because, in the absence of one, another can be incomplete. Without segmentation, targeting is not possible, and if there is no targeting, there is no need of market segmentation (Dibb and Simkin, 2008). A market is the sum of different types of customers, and all of them may not be the potential customers of an organisation. Dividing them into various segments and identifying the most suitable target customer segment is understood as market segmentation and targeting. An organisation might have multiple products and services, and they can be sold in numerous market segments. A proper targeting determines specific products/services for the particular market segment. Dibb and Simkin (2008) say that market segmentation helps an organisation for developing a planning to outsource raw materials, manufacturing products, buying products, storing products, managing staffs, managing financial resources and marketing products. It clarifies that targeting helps an organisation to manage its business activities effectively and to fulfil its strategic objectives. For instance, if a dairy organisation is producing whole milk, its target market might be the customers who use the whole milk. It helps the organisation to determine market demand, human resource, storage capacity, target profit and the required quantity of milk.

A great business plan includes market segmentation and targeting because it is one of the critical strategic factors to succeed an organisation in achieving strategic objectives. If an organisation tries to sell whole milk in the market where most of the consumers want semi-skimmed milk, it is difficult to sell. In simple term, market segmentation divides the entire market into workable segments, whereas targeting helps to select the most suitable segment(s). The more market is divided into smaller segments, the more suitable segment(s) can be identified. An organisation might have limitations of time and resources; thereby, it may not be able to address the needs of every single sector. Lack of clarity in market segment might create a type of vagueness in identifying geographical location, product/service types, price and promotion. The market can be broadly segmented into four types:

- Demographic segmentation
- Behavioural segmentation
- Psychological segmentation
- Geographical segmentation

2.4.1. Demographic Segmentation

Demographic segmentation is often used to draft a business plan. According to Boone and Kurtz (2014), this is a significant segmentation type as it acknowledges organisation various factors of the population including age, gender, income, race, nationality, education, religion, family size, and occupation. Based on these factors, the people can be further divided into different sub-segments. Based on the organisation's products and services, the most suitable market segment type can be selected. For example, if an organisation is planning to sell meat, then demographic segmentation might be required under which religious sub-section should be carried out. Muslim religious people eat only Halal meat; Hindu religious people do not eat beef as they pray cow as goddess, and Christian religious people love to eat beef. If the market is divided based on religion, then the most suitable target group can be identified. Here, it is not possible to target all religious people; for example, if Hindu knows the shop also sells beef, then he does not want to buy meat from that shop. Here, segmentation acknowledges statistic of different religious customers and helps to find the most suitable target group(s) and to develop the most appropriate strategies.

2.4.2. Behavioural Segmentation

Consumer behaviour determines a customer's buying decision-making process. Dolnicar, Grun and Leisch (2018) say that behavioural segment helps to understand consumers' needs and desires. Different people might have their priorities, and they behave accordingly. Based on product or service, this segmentation can be divided into further sub-segmentations. As, automobile industry can divide the market like walker/cycle rider, public transport users, and private transport users (ordinary, medium and sophisticated) which depicts the market behaviour of the commuters. If there are more ordinary customers, the automobile may prefer to produce average vehicles instead of advanced. Such type of behavioural sub-segments can be made by every business to pick up the most suitable segment(s) and to focus its activities accordingly.

2.4.3. Psychographic Segmentation

Psychographic segment is associated with attribute, psychology, attitude, interest, opinion, motivation, personality and lifestyle of the consumer. As behavioural segment, it also emphasises consumer activities. But it tries to define each business activities from a psychological point of view. It finds out the underlying essences in the segment, and that could be used as a framework to explain similar actions. For example, if a particular customer has an attraction in traditional activities; it can be imagined that she/he may not be interested in the latest fashion clothing. As the market is understood through psychographic segmentation, an organisation can know the products and services that are required to fulfil their needs (Maslow, 1970). Based on the consumer psychology, an organisation can sub-segment consumers into different groups. For example, a clothing store can segment the market based on lifestyle, whereas a sugar factory can segment the market based on the market's attitude on using sugar. Same type of psychographic segmentation may not be applicable for each organisation. It is due to they have different nature in term of their products and services.

2.4.4. Geographic Segmentation

Geographic segmentation is also one of the critical market segmentation types. It divides entire market into different groups based on the geography in which they reside like rural and urban area, hilly and plain area, remote and central area, rich and deprived area, cold and hot area, and so on. This kind of segmentation gives an excellent insight into the particular area, and suitable product/service can be easily determined (Grun and Leisch, 2018). For example, if the domain is deprived, the customer purchasing ability cannot be high; so, the cheaper products or services should be targeted at that market.

2.5. Selection of Products/Services

An organisation requires to select the most suitable products and services to sell in the market. Here, the question may arouse - how to determine the most suitable products or services. It is not an easy job because it requires market research which costs much time, money and effort. Regarding the selection process, one has to conduct a market research to find out the market needs and has to design better products or services than available in the market. If an organisation offers the same type of products or services that the competitors have been already selling, it is impossible to secure a sustainable competitive advantage (Porter, 1985). At present, there might be several choices to the customers; so, to attract more customers, an organisation has to offer something different. According to Reynolds and Lancaster (2007), target customers' expectation and products' available in the market are the key aspects that contribute to determine the right products and services. While deciding such products or services, an organisation has to conduct feasibility test in which an organisation has to consider issues like cost, resources and timing factors. For example, if the production cost of the particular product is too high, but target customers have low dispensable income, then such product cannot be sold in that market. So, an organisation should be clear on its target market, production cost, production time, price, infrastructure, employees' skills, sales quantity, profitability, investment, financial resources and potential impacts on the target market. If all of these factors are properly considered while determining the products/services, an organisation can be successful in fulfilling its strategic objectives. There are five key ways by which an organisation can determine the most suitable products/services to sell in the market.

- Identification of the target market
- Market research
- Selection of products/services
- Product test
- Improvement as required

2.5.1. Identification of the Target Market

In the market, there might be several segments, and it is not easy to cover all of them by an organisation due to time, cost and resource limitations. Also, from sales and profitability management perspectives targeting an entire market is not suitable. For example, if there are only a few customers who love a particular product, it is difficult to produce such product because it costs much money and effort than its return. If there is no growth opportunity, and it cannot cover even the cost, there is no meaning of producing such product. Each segment may want different product to fulfil their distinct needs and desires (Grun and Leisch, 2018). If an organisation intends to produce various products, then focus will be distracted. It means to say that financial resources, human resources, time and effort can be divided; so, the organisation faces difficulties to enhance quality. In the competitive market environment, an organisation should have something extraordinary than the market to achieve competitive advantage. If the product is similar to the alternative products, the customers do not buy it. In this regard, the products should be better and innovative than the products sold by the competitors. As discussed in market segmentation and targeting, the entire market should be divided into different sub-segments as per the nature of the products. For example, a local pizza shop can segment the market based on demographic segmentation because religion, family size, and income can be the key determining factors. Based on the demographic segmentation, the entire market can be sub-divided into various groups, and the most suitable segment(s) can be selected.

2.5.2. Market Research

Based on the target market, extensive market research should be carried out to collect an intensive insight into the target market. In such research, several factors such as customers' economic condition, competition, market needs and desires, legal factors and environmental aspects have to be considered. It helps to determine the most suitable product, price, place, promotion and many more. Gupta (2004) says that if there is no market research, it is difficult to identify customers' needs and desires, competition and economic situation of the target customers. Both primary and secondary data can be collected and used in the research as required. Secondary data can be collected from books, journals, articles, newspapers, presentation papers and various websites. And the primary data can be obtained directly through the sample respondents using different data collection instruments such as interview, questionnaire, focus group, observation, case study and role-playing.

2.5.3. Selection of Products/services

There might be several suitable products and their alternatives that may fit in the target market. But an organisation has to identify the most suitable products/services based on the feasibility factors like infrastructure, required employees' skill, sales quantity, target profit, required investment and financial resource of the organisation. For example, if the organisation has limited finance and particular product requires higher investment, it may not be feasible to produce that product. To offer some specific products, employees may require specific skills. And if an organisation cannot develop such skills, it cannot produce such product.

2.5.4. Product Test

As the product is produced, it should not be directly sent in the market because it may need some further improvements to which product test can be imperative. The customers make their impression on the particular product or service from their first use. If a new product is launched in the market with some flaws, it can create a negative impact on the products. If the customers have a negative impression, it severely affects the organisation's image, and it cannot compete in the market (Schmitt, 2011). In this sense, before sending the products in the market, the sample products should be tested from the potential customers. While testing the product, the organisation should be careful in collecting as accurate as possible information. If there is a researcher's influence, the customers' feedbacks cannot be fair. For instance, if a restaurant offers a free meal for the food testing purpose, and the manager asks feedback of the food, mostly the customers cannot complain as they have received free food and service. This kind of method cannot collect objective data. But if several customers are invited in the food testing event and asked them to drop their feedback anonymously into the letterbox, they can express their experience. The product test acknowledges organisation to what extent the product is going to fulfil the needs and desires of the target customers, and it helps to identify strengths and weaknesses of the product.

2.5.5. Improvement as Required

As the product is tested, the feedback is used to understand its strengths and weaknesses. The advantages can be continued whereas the defects can be noticed and effectively rectified to which it may require some extra time, effort and investment. But its impacts on the market can be huge because it can contribute to increase customers' satisfaction level and the organisation's image. If the products or services are sent in the market with some defects, in the competitive market, it will create a long last negative impression. So, this phase is equally important to produce successful products or services.

2.6. Aim and Objectives

Aim is an ultimate goal/destination that the business organisation wants to achieve. It helps an organisation to determine the right strategy and to control and monitor every activity of an organisation. The management in the business organisation is responsible for determining the aim and for making each stakeholder clear about it. An organisation without purpose means losing the control of the competitive market. An organisation can have a single aim for multiple objectives. For example, a restaurant's target could be "to be a number one restaurant in its market." To fulfil this aim, it can have several objectives like "to increase the number of loyal customers," "to offer highly tasty and hygienic food," "to provide quality service," "to satisfy needs and desires in a better way," and many more.

Aim is long term goal which is supported by objectives. Also, the aim is presented in general form and objective specifies the target. It indicates that the objective is the supplement part of the aim. In other words, the aim is the overall purpose of the organisation and goals have to be formulated based on aim. Aim is a general outcome under which several short term outcomes can be formulated. Merely setting objective does not help an organisation to fulfil its aim because vague and impractical objective cannot be achieved, and it will not have any positive impacts to the organisation. So, question may arouse what kind of objectives help an organisation to fulfil its aim. The answer is simple - the SMART objectives help to fulfil aim as it ensures the effectiveness of the objectives (Drucker, 1955). SMART stands for five significant attributes such as specific, measurable, achievable, realistic and timely (time-bound). As the objective secures these attributes, it can be useful to fulfil the organisation's aim. And those attributes are briefly described as follows:

A. Specific

Specific indicates to particular, definite or narrowed down objective. It is precise or accurate; a clear statement that should point out the intended outcome or achievement. Any vague purpose cannot be fulfilled, and further, it cannot motivate organisation (Doran, 1981). It means to say that any imprecise objective does not contribute an organisation to direct it in the right direction and to succeed in achieving a competitive market environment. While developing objectives, it is better to use action verbs like analyse, identify, differentiate, and test. And to make the goals more specific, they should be presented in rate, number, percentage and frequency if it is possible.

B. Measurable

An objective should always be measurable; so that, the progress can be monitored (Doran, 1981). There must be a particular method, system, technique or procedure that should identify the level of achievement. For example, if an organisation has an objective as "to increase annual profit" it is not measurable since it does not point the target. Here, it is not clear what percentage or what amount is expected to increase. This objective is not measurable as the progress cannot also be monitored. The measurable objective could "to increase annual profit by 20%" where the target is clear, and it can be measured to what per cent it has become successful.

C. Achievable

Objective should be achievable; otherwise, it will be like a daydream which cannot assist an organisation in fulfilling strategic objectives. While developing an objective, practicality issues should be considered, which means to say that with a reasonable effort, it should be achieved. Doran (1981) states that while setting an objective, an organisation has to review resources, time, measurability, and limitations. If an objective becomes unachievable, it cannot increase motivation. For example, if a car has a maximum speed of 120 miles per hour, but the target is set to drive 140 miles per hour. In this situation, it is impossible to achieve such objective. And the driver does not even try to make it. But if the objective is to drive in 115 miles per hour, it is achievable, and it would help to "reach destination on time."

D. Realistic

A good objective has to emphases on outcome instead of method or approach. Instruments are merely the means, and they do not have much impact on outcome, but it does not mean that they can be ignored. They are equally essential to achieve an objective, but the primary focus should be given on the outcome as it contributes to fulfil strategic aims and objectives of the organisation. Only a realistic target can take into account resources to achieve goals (Doran, 1981). Both human and financial resources should be considered while determining an objective. If the resources do not support, then the objective cannot be achieved, and such an objective may not have any positive impact on the organisation. Unrealistic objective cannot produce a positive outcome, and it will be merely wastage of time, effort and investment; thereby, while developing any objective, it should be evaluated whether it is realistic or not.

E. Timely (time-bound)

A good objective has to indicate practical time duration by which the outcome should be achieved. As the deadline or date is fixed, it helps to measure the progress of the objective. For example, if a particular goal is expected to complete within a year, in six months, almost half of the job should be completed. If the average expected target is not completed, it requires to change its strategies or increase speed. If the deadline is not set, progress cannot be measured, and effective planning cannot be developed. Further, it can take a long time if there is no time-bound, and it will increase cost, time and effort. Besides, if it takes a long time, the effect of the outcome cannot be as useful and practical as much as it would be on time. Time-bound creates urgency in action, helps to develop a plan and motivates people who are responsible for accomplishing the objective (Doran, 1981). While creating a target, one should carry out a tentative measurement in relation with time duration. Each outcome associated with the objectives should be given appropriate time. Further, possible limitations should also be brought into consideration while setting time duration for the particular target.

Every organisation, team, or individual has to develop a SMART objective to direct each activity in the right direction. SMART framework contributes to create specific, measurable, achievable, realistic and time-bound targets. Here, aims and objectives should not be firm because along with changes in the internal and external environmental factors of an organisation, some adjustments may always be required.

2.7. Resources

Resource in business organisation refers to any asset that can be used to function business activities effectively. It might be some sources, supplies or stocks which have a crucial role to operate any organisation. Without proper resources, operations cannot be performed effectively and cannot meet the target. Medina (2006) says that there are different types of resources, but from a business perspective, they can be studied under two broad types: financial resource and human resource. To effectively run any business organisation, both types of resources are equally necessary, and they are complementary to each other. For example, if the employees are not skilful, merely proper infrastructure, adequate finance and quality raw material cannot be enough to fulfil the strategic objectives of an organisation. Also, if other resources are weak, only employees' skills and abilities do not help the organisation to fulfil its strategic objectives.

2.7.1. Financial Resources

Any service or asset that is associated with the economy can be understood as a financial resource. It includes both monetary and non-monetary supply or stock that is used to perform business activities. It is the backbone of the business because, without financial resources, no business activity can be imagined. It is necessary for different purposes: machinery, lands and buildings, raw materials, goods and services, interest on loans, rents, wages and other infrastructures.

A. Machinery

Based on the organisation's nature, different types of machines might be required to operate business activities to which finance is essential. A business may need some types of machinery which can be arranged either by purchasing or renting, but in both ways, it costs some amounts. For example, if someone is trying to establish a restaurant, kitchen items like micro-oven, blender, refrigerator and others can be the required machineries. To manage them, the restaurant must be financially capable.

B. Land and Buildings

Lands and buildings are the places where business activities take places. Every property or structure that is used for business purpose must be managed by the organisation to which finance is required (Broadbent and Cullen, 2012). In case of restaurant any parking space, kitchen room, bathroom, reception area, bar and dining room may come under this category. Most of the organisations use land and buildings on rent as it saves a massive amount of financial investment. It can be taken in contract for a specified time duration, and it can be renewable. If an organisation uses them on rent, more capital can be used for growth and development of the business. In the same way, it is imperative to say that if the business is not doing well in particular location, it can quickly move to the suitable place, but as it has bought the land or building, then it will not be that much easy to sell them and move.

C. Raw Materials

Raw materials are the essential materials to produce a particular product. It is not saleable in the market as it is; they should be processed and converted to the finished products. Raw materials are cheaper, but as they are proceeded and made saleable in the market, its price can be higher. Labour cost, profit, energy cost and other costs can be added to determine the price of the finished product. Mishra (2009) says that raw materials need a significant portion of the finance and based on business, different types of raw materials might be required. In the case of the restaurant, raw materials like meat, chicken, vegetable, floor, rice and many more are needed. Some of the suppliers can give raw materials in credit, and after processing and selling, the organisation can pay that credit. If any raw materials are available in such term, its financial burden can be reduced. But every raw material may not be available in that term; so that, financial resource should be arranged.

D. Goods and Services

An organisation may not be able to produce each and everything. It can buy some of the products to complement its product portfolio. Some of the organisations directly buy the finished products and sell in the markets. Grocery stores directly buy the finished goods and sell in the market. They do not produce any product; they entirely depend upon suppliers. They buy, store and sell to the final customers. But, in a restaurant, products like wine, beer, coke and others are purchased from the market as they are not produced at the restaurant. To buy such goods, an organisation needs finance. Also, as per required, an organisation can outsource services to perform activities. For such services, an organisation has to pay money. In the case of restaurant organisation, it can buy different services such as marketing, legal support and computer software service from the market.

E. Interest on Loan

Some of the organisations might have a business loan, and they have to pay interest on it, to which finance is necessary. Most of the organisations manage interest from day to day business activities, but if the sales level is low, it may require to maintain interest from other financial sources (Mishra, 2009). For example, if the start-up business has a bank loan, it may not generate profit in the first month, but it has to pay the interest from the first month to which it has to manage finance from different sources.

F. Rent

Some of the business organisations have their land and buildings to perform business activities. But others may not have their own; so, they have to use rented property which can be available in contract for a particular time duration, and it can be renewable as well. As per the agreement, rent has to be paid; mostly, it can be paid yearly basis. To pay this kind of expense, an organisation needs financial resources. If an organisation has a problem in paying such rent, then business activities cannot be effectively functioned (Santucci, 2013). Instead of focusing on business performance, the management has to concentrate on managing rent because if it is not paid on time, the owner can shut the business down through legal action.

G. Wages

Usually, in the family-run businesses, every activity has to be handled by the members of the family. Thereby, they do not need to pay any wages. Still, some of the family-run businesses recruit few employees from the labour market to support the business activities, and they have to pay salaries. In some charity organisations, people work as unpaid volunteers. But most other organisations pay wages to each employee, that is a significant portion of business expenses (Mishra, 2009). If the organisation is doing well, such expense can be managed by its profit, but if there is no profit, it has to be managed with some additional sources. It tries to clarify that to pay employees' wages, financial resources are required. If a restaurant has 12 full-time employees, it has to pay their wages weekly or monthly basis as per the contract sign. It does not matter whether the restaurant is in profit or loss. It has to manage such payments from any source. If wages are not paid on time, the employees do not work, and the organisation cannot fulfil its strategic objectives.

H. Other Infrastructures

Based on business nature, different infrastructures may require to effectively and efficiently function business activities. For example, a restaurant may require furniture, vehicle for food delivery, oven and many more. It requires financial resources to manage those infrastructures. Mostly, they are managed during the start-up phase, and some of them can be arranged in the course of business operation. For example, if the oven is not working, it has to be changed, and if extra chairs are required, they have to be managed. Managing infrastructure while operating business activities can be easier because it can be managed by revenue or profit.

2.7.2. Human Resources

Human resource (HR) is considered as any human skill, ability or energy that is used to perform business activities. An involvement of human being in the business activities can be understood as the use of HR. It can be both physical and mental contribution, but it must require a proper HR to fulfil business objectives. Human resource management (HRM) is responsible for recruiting the right candidates for the right job and for exploring their optimum potentialities.

If an organisation has capable and qualified employees, it can easily fulfil its strategic objectives by outperforming the competitors (Porter, 1985). Considering this fact, every organisation has been giving much more emphasis on HRM. Before establishing an organisation, the management has to determine how many employees and what kinds of skills are required. If it is known in advance, it makes the recruitment process more manageable and effective. As the employees are capable of performing their roles and responsibilities, they can be motivated to their job; and their performance can be highly qualitative.

2.8. Sources of Finance

An organisation requires finance for different purposes including wages, interest on loans, rents, machinery, raw materials and bills. It can be managed using several sources which can be studied under two broad categories: internal and external sources.

2.8.1. Internal Source

Internal source of finance indicates to achieving the required finance from within the organisation. This type of source is easy to arrange as it has an organisation's control. Also, it does not need to be repaid, and no interest is payable. Due to these advantages, the management is free from financial burden; so, it can fully concentrate over business performance (Rigby, 2011). By using this source, an organisation can collect limited finance and every organisation may not be equally able to arrange this source because it depends upon the nature of the organisation and owner's financial strength. There are several internal sources such as owner's investment, retained earnings, sales of stock, sales of fixed assets and debt collection.

2.8.1.1. Owner's Investment

Owner's investment indicates to the capital or economy that comes from owner's savings which can be used to start-up or to extend a business organisation. If the business type is partnership, there will be two or more than two owners who can invest their savings. But in case of single owner, all of the investment should be managed by oneself. If there is high investment but limited saving, most of the investors go in partnership; therefore, the capital can be increased as well as business risk can be decreased (shared). According to Rigby (2011) as this type of finance is arranged by the owner(s), it is not required to pay back within one year which means to say that it is a long-term source of finance.

2.8.1.2. Retained Earnings

Retained earnings refer to re-investing business profit for its growth and development. For start-up businesses, this kind of resource cannot be available. When the company trades for more than one year and earns some profit, this type of resource can be used. The organisation re-invests the profit in the same business instead of sharing it to the investors or shareholders. It can re-invest either total profit or some portion as required. Some organisations pay some part of the profit to the investors and remaining re-invest in the business. If all of the profit is invested, it de-motivates the investors. So, sharing at least a small portion of the profit can be more fruitful from the investor point of view.

Retained earnings allow owner(s) a full control of business because it does not add any creditors, new partners or outside investors. This kind of resource can be understood as a medium or long term source of finance because the organisation does not need to pay it quickly back or within one year. And no interest is payable on the retained earnings. As it is re-invested, the shareholders' share value will be increased (Bhat, 2008). Also, as the business is limited within this option, there may not be sufficient finance which may trigger the risk of losing investment opportunities.

Further, some cash should be balanced for day to day business operation, but if all of the profit is re-invested, there will be a problem in managing ongoing operations as well. Besides, this kind of source has to pay double tax: corporate tax and shareholder tax. For example, if an organisation has £40,000 profit, it has to pay 20% corporate tax (8,000) on it and earnings per share can be determined. If there are 32 shares, each share earns £1,000 as the profit, and if an investor has 15 shares, his income will be £15,000. And he has to pay personal income tax on it which can be 20% on the total income after deducting personal allowance. No matter whether profit is distributed to shareholders or retained by the organisation, personal income tax must be paid; so that, this source of finance has to pay double tax.

2.8.1.3. Sales of Stock

Sales of stock can also be one of the internal sources of finance. If an organisation has some stock or unsold products, they can be sold off to generate funding for further investment. As the particular product becomes successful to meet the expected profit, the remaining stocks can be quickly sold in offer to collect finance. This sort of finance is required to operate day to day business activities; thereby, it can be considered as a short-term source of finance (Dlabay and Burrow, 2007). For a quick sale, it should reduce the price that may decrease the revenue and profitability, but by selling it, the stock holding cost will be decreased. This type of source may not be available for the start-up business as well as for the existing business that does not have stock products in the store.

2.8.1.4. Sales of Fixed Assets

Some of the unused fixed assets like land, machinery and building which are no longer needed for an organisation could be sold and used the finance for additional investment. Bank loan or overdraft is one of the best ways of funding because it mobilises still capital. Also, the organisation does not need to pay back this amount or pay interest on it (Stickney, Weil and Schipper, 2009). It is a medium-term source of finance. But it is imperative to say that an organisation might have very limited or nothing such unused fixed assets. In such situation, it is not a relevant source of finance. Further, this type of source is minimal; thereby, it may not be able to manage the required amount of investment. And even if there are unused assets, managing finance from this method is very difficult because those assets cannot be sold quickly and easily.

2.8.1.5. Debt Collection

Debt is the amount that is owed by the debtors. An organisation can have various debtors from whom the finance can be collected. Stickney, Weil and Schipper (2009) say that debt collection is the process of obtaining the company's money which was owned by someone else. Debt might be, sometimes, in the risk of not being recovered, which is called bad debt. This type of financial resource is highly beneficial as it collects almost wastage like amount and reinvests in the business. It is a part of the regular operation of the company. Debt should be effectively monitored and received on time to run day to day activities. This type of resource is considered a short-term source of finance. Debt collection reduces the risk of increasing bad debt (Hedges, Levy and Proud, 2007). Also, this type of finance should not be paid back, and no interest is payable. But it is imperative to say that every organisation may not have debtors, and there might be a minimal amount which triggers missing significant investment opportunities.

2.8.2. External Source

External source of finance is the capital that is managed from outside the organisation. Compared to an internal source, it requires extensive documentation, and it is difficult to manage as well. This source can collect a huge amount of finance, but it depends on the business situation or its owner(s). As per the nature of the business organisation, different sources of finance can be available. There are eight key external sources of finance like bank loan or overdraft, additional partners, share issue, leasing, hire purchase, mortgage, trade credit and government grant.

2.8.2.1. Bank Loan or Overdraft

It is one of the popular external sources of finance, which is issued by the bank or banking society for certain time duration at an agreed rate of interest and fee. It can be available for start-up as well as established businesses. Coyle (2002) says that bank loan can be used as long or medium-term finance, but overdraft can be short-term finance because overdraft fee can be higher and it is only supposed to use in an urgent case and payback as soon as possible. To get a bank loan or overdraft approval, an organisation should have a good credit history, well-reputation and higher profitability, which is not possible for a start-up business. As the bank loan or overdraft is used, it has to be repaid based on agreed repayment spread (instalment). Such instalment helps an organisation to manage money easily. But, it can be expensive for a long run because it has to pay the interest on debt or overdraft for a long time which reduces the organisation's profit.

2.8.2.2. Additional Partners

Sometimes, a business organisation can increase the number of partners if it requires some extra fund for its expansion. It is, basically, suitable for the partnership business type in which new partner(s) can be included to collect some extra finance. According to Hillman and Loewenstein (2015) by adding partner(s), the owner increases not only capital but also knowledge, experience and expertise. Besides, potential financial risk can also be shared among the partners. The major advantages of this type of capital are: it should not be repaid, there is no interest, and it can be used as long term capital. It has some disadvantages, which are: difficulty in the decision-making process; feeling of low responsibilities of the partners and the profit is divided.

2.8.2.3. Share Issue

Both private and public companies can issue share to raise their capital. Unlike public companies, private companies cannot trade their shares on a public exchange, and they cannot issue through an initial public offering. Walton and Aerts (2006) argue that a company might have several shares, and the market determines their price. It can be most suitable for the limited company. In case of advantages, this kind of finance is not required to be repaid, and no interest is payable on it. And it can be understood as a long term source of finance. But along with issuing share, the profit should be paid for each share as a dividend. As a disadvantage, the decision-making process can be complicated due to the multiple shareholders.

2.8.2.4. Leasing

Leasing is the process of obtaining the required asset without paying an upfront lump sum amount. The payment can be spread into instalment, which makes an organisation easy to manage its day to day activities and pay lease instalment. Although it is good for budgeting, over the long run, it can be expensive, and the asset belongs to the finance company

(Boobyer, 2003). A finance company can arrange leasing, and it has to fulfil certain documentation for legal purpose. At first, the organisation has to pay some initial amount and the fee of the financial company. If the asset is expensive, it might be difficult to get finance because the financial company checks paying back capacity to determine whether to accept or decline the leasing request. It can be considered as the medium-term source of finance.

2.8.2.5. Hire Purchase

Hire purchase indicates to buying assets in instalment basis. Similar to leasing, this source of finance allows an opportunity for the organisation to use the required infrastructures without investing a lump sum. In the beginning, a certain deposit amount should be paid, and the rest of the amount can be settled in instalment basis. As the amount can be paid in instalment basis, the organisation does not need to settle the full amount in advance. And it also does not need more documentation; thereby, an organisation can easily manage the required asset, but in the long run, it can be costly compared to buying with down payment. It is a medium source of finance (Dransfield, 2005).

2.8.2.6. Mortgage

Mortgage is a secured loan that is available on land or building offered by the financial society. This type of loan can be paid an instalment basis; thereby, it can be considered as the long term loan. In the same way, as it is secured loan, its interest can be cheaper, and as the full payment is made, the business owns the property, but until the full amount is paid, the property will be in the name of banking society that offered the loan (Kolbe, Greer and Rudner, 2003). This source of finance is good for budgeting point of view because the business organisation can have the required land or building with a minimum amount of money. Further, it can be paid in a long term instalment basis which helps to manage the finance effectively. But over the long run, the business has to pay more amount than buying in cash. In the same way, if the business does not become able to pay the instalment, it will create a huge loss because the financing company can sell the property on auction to recover its money. At that time, the business might lose its initial deposit amount as well as the instalments that were paid.

2.8.2.7. Trade Credit

Trade credit refers to buying the products or services in credit for a short term. It is similar to the concept of "buy now and pay later." In the competitive market environment, suppliers use this strategy to sell their products or services in the market. Pandey (2015) says that the total sum of this kind of credit can be considered as trade credit. It can be used for a short time duration, mostly 30 days; thereby, it is a short term source of finance. Business can get products or services without paying the cost in advance, but it should be paid after making the sales. It helps business organisation to run its day to day business activities in low cash flow. Also, if the credit is paid on time, there will not be any extra fee and interest on the credit. But in trade credit, the suppliers may not give any discount. In the market, the competitors might get it at a discounted price as they do down payment which makes trade credit products or services costly and makes difficult to compete in the competitive market environment.

2.8.2.8. Government Grants

Government grant is a government's finance which is available for both start-up as well as established businesses but to get such grant they have to meet certain criteria set by the government. For example, if any organisation has been using solar energy, the government might give a certain amount as a grant. Because using solar energy is more environment-friendly, and it reduces dependency on foreign oil, creates jobs and reduces foreign business loss. Morris, McKay and Oates (2009) say that this source of finance should not be paid back, and there is no interest on it. But every organisation may not be eligible to receive grant, and there might be lots of terms and conditions which might be difficult to fulfil.

2.9. Determining a Suitable Source of Finance

As describe above, there are several internal and external sources of finance, but each source may not be equally applicable to a business organisation. Using the wrong source of funding may increase the cost of the organisation, and it may create difficulties in managing financial resources; thereby, it is imperative to select the right source of finance. To ensure the right source of funding, an organisation could consider some aspects like type of business, required amount, purpose and time factor.

2.9.1. Type of Business

Different types of companies might have their unique attributes or features, which can be used as the critical issues in determining the right choice of financial source. For instance, a sole proprietorship cannot offer shares to collect capital investment unlike a public company. Mostly, this kind of business uses the owner's savings, loan/credit or trade credit that depends upon the availability.

2.9.2. Required Amount

Some of the sources of finance may have limitations in collecting the amount (Ketkar and Ratha, 2008). For example, debt collection can be regarded as a minimal source of funding because an organisation may not have many debtors to collect a significant amount of money. Further, it not suitable for the start-up business. But share issue source of finance can collect a considerable amount. Similarly, a public organisation can sell its shares in the public market on stock exchange to obtain a substantial amount. But if it requires only a little amount, it can either use debt collection, sales of stock, loan, trade credit or leasing, as per required.

2.9.3. Purpose

Some of the sources of finance are designed for a specific use. For instance, mortgage is only available for buying either land or building. Similarly, leasing and hire purchase are designed to facilitate equipment. If an organisation needs investment for marketing a particular product or service, these kinds of sources will not be suitable. Thus, based on the purpose, a business organisation has to determine the most appropriate source of finance.

2.9.4. Time Factor

Finance can be divided into three types based on time factor: short, medium and long. If it is required for less than five years (in some cases less than one year), it can be considered as short term finance, and there are numbers of short term sources of funding such as sales of stock, debt collection and trade credit. In the same way, if it is required for more than five years but less than ten years, it can be considered as the medium-term finance which can be managed by different sources like sale of fixed assets, leasing, hire purchase and loan. Finally, if the organisation needs the amount for a more extended period than ten years, it can be understood as long term finance. And it can be managed by different sources like mortgage, share, owner's investment, long term loan, additional partner(s) and government grant.

CHAPTER 3

Thriving in the Competitive Market Environment

3.1. Customers are the Business Hub

Customers are the axis of any business organisation in the 21st century. The more an organisation satisfies the needs and desires of its target customers, the more it can be successful in fulfilling its strategic objectives. Without a doubt, today, a customer has lots of choices in the market; thereby, she/he selects the products/services that best satisfy her/his needs and desires. It clarifies that as the business organisation becomes able to meet customers' needs and wants better than the competitors, it can easily attract and retain the customers.

Different customer segments might have various priorities. For example, some customers might be looking for cheaper products; some others for qualitative or better products; some other for innovative products and some other for more reliable products. An organisation has to identify customers' needs and desires, and they should be properly addressed if it wants to sustain in the competitive market environment (Porter, 1985). Customers' needs and desires cannot be firm; they are in the motion of perpetual change. In this regard, an organisation has to conduct market research in every six months and bring changes in strategic issues as required. Using market feedback and brining necessary changes keeps on a business organisation alive. If customers' expectations are not identified, the business cannot sustain in the market.

3.2. Competitive Strategies

Establishing a company means to enter into the competitive market environment. Thousands of business organisations come into the market, but all of them may not be equally successful in achieving their strategic objectives because of the harsh competitive market environment. Here, the primary concern is in sustaining the business instead of merely establishing. An organisation has to develop its competitive approaches to continue in the competitive market environment.

Competitive strategy indicates a long term planning of an organisation that helps to outperform its competitors and gain additional strengths. In the competition, only the fittest companies survive and others extinct from the market. Along with increasing competition and developing information technologies, competition has become so harsh; therefore, every business organisation attempts to find a defensive position. Repeating the same thing and expecting a new result is a mistake that some of the organisations commit. It means to say that doing similar thing like other organisations does not ensure competitive strength; it requires to do something extra that the other companies have not done. To develop the most suitable competitive strategies, Porter's competitive framework, and Gray and Balmer's (1998) corporate identity might be the supportive concepts.

3.2.1. Porter's Competitive Strategies

Porter (1985) says, "Competition is at the core of success or failure of firms." This statement tries to clarify that an organisation's success is not only related to its performance; it is compared to the competitors, and only the better organisations ensure success. Porter's generic strategy says that an organisation can use three approaches: cost leadership, differentiation and focus (figure 4).

Competitive Scope	Lower Cost	Differentiation
Broad Target	1. Cost Leadership	2. Differentiation
Narrow Target	3A. Cost Focus	3B. Differentiation Focus

Figure 4: Competitive advantage

A. Cost Leadership

Cost leadership indicates to producing products or services at a cheaper cost than the cost of its competitors. Porter (1985) says that being a low-cost producer in the industry is understood as the cost leadership. Here, a query may arise how could a company produce similar quality products or services at a lower cost. Answer of this question is not that much easy because if it would be so easy, every organisation would quickly become the low-cost producer, and no cost advantage would exist with any organisation. In the name of saving cost, an organisation should not compromise in quality and quantity because it dissatisfies target customers.

There are numbers of factors that directly or indirectly affect supply chain management of an organisation. Supply chain is directly associated with the cost of the products or services; thereby, an organisation needs to exploit each factor in the optimum level. Cheaper financial capital, highly skilful HR, cheaper raw material, effective technology, and efficient marketing are the key factors that help an organisation to achieve cost leadership. If an organisation operates business activities at a cheaper cost than the average cost and sustains it for a long time, it can make extra advantage in the industry (Porter, 1985).

Cost leadership increases numbers of loyal customers (by selling products or services at a lower price)or profitability (by selling at the market price). If it sells at a lower price, it increases the number of customers and revenue as well. It will have more satisfied and loyal customers that helps it to generate more profit, create better brand image, predict sales and develop effective planning. Also, if it sells in a competitive or market price, its profit will be higher than the benefit of the competitors. Although it sells less quantity, its profit will be higher. Based on the nature of business and market situation, an organisation can decide either to sell at a lower price or in the market price (Porter, 1985). For example, at the time of economic recession, the customers may not have adequate dispensable income. So, their concerns will on saving the amount; thereby, at that time selling products or services at a lower price could be better. But, if an organisation has a very congested area where it cannot accommodate more customers as well as it cannot increase its product quantity, selling at the market price could be more suitable.

Cost leadership should be sustainable because if it does not sustain for a long term, then no competitive advantage may exist. If the competitors can easily copy the strategy or if the applied technology can be replaced by the better one, cost leadership cannot be sustained. So, the policy or technology must be challenging to imitate. Aldi, a German grocery chain, has been using a cost leadership strategy. And to exploit the cost, it has been producing more private-label brands, offering a limited selection of products, keeping limited stock, using low labour cost and focusing on efficient human resource. It means to say that it has been exploiting cost leadership through several factors and imitating all of those things by its competitors is not an easy task because it requires a significant amount of investment and much effort.

B. Differentiation

According to Porter (1985), "In a differentiation strategy, a firm seeks to be unique in its industry along some dimensions that are widely valued by buyers." It is the quality of being different than the competitors, but merely different does not ensure competitive advantage; it must add some value to the product or service. An organisation seeks to be unique through one or more than one attributes. Differentiating strategy costs much time, effort and money because it is a new practice. But in return the organisation can be rewarded by price premium which means to say that it can sell products or services at a higher price and if that uniquely fulfils customers' needs and desires, they do not mind to pay extra amount.

An organisation has to conduct adequate research, use new technology, train staffs and apply new techniques while implementing differentiation strategy. And as it is unique, risk can also be equally associated. There are different sectors like product, marketing, place, process, and so on. And an organisation can bring differentiation in one or more than one sections. Even in the particular sector, partial distinction can also be made (Thmopson and Martin, 2005). For example, iPhone X and iPhone XS are two different series which have partial differences, especially in display, performance and camera. But there is no difference in design, software and operating system. Here, it has been differentiating its product with the previous version, and by adding some additional features, it competes with other competitors like Samsung, Oppo, Huawei, Asus, Sony and others. No matter whether it is entire or partial differentiation, it has to fulfil the needs and desires of the target market to achieve competitive advantage.

Differentiation should be difficult to imitate by its competitors; so, the competitive advantage can sustain longer. If it is easy to copy or achieve in less effort, every competitor might get it, and no competitive advantage may exist. Also, if the differentiation becomes less critical to the buyers, again, the competitive advantage does not sustain for long-lasting. Today, customers' needs and desires have been perpetually changing; competition has been increasing and technological development has been heightening day by day. Due to these reasons, competitive advantage achieved through differentiation strategy is in perpetual threat of dismantle.

C. Focus

Focus is a narrow competitive scope which "selects a particular segment or group of segments in the industry" (Porter, 1985) as the target market. As there is a narrow market, the organisation can better understand customers' needs and desires. This strategy tries to satisfy customers and create a niche market. Here, significant weight is gained through the difference between a focuser's target segment and other segments in the industry (Porter, 1985). It means to say that this strategy considerably concentrates over peculiar segment in the market that has not been adequately addressed by the "broadly-targeted competitors." This strategy will be only applicable if the customers have unique needs, or the production and delivery system extraordinarily fulfils target customers' needs and desires. The advantage achieved from this strategy will be lost as soon as the peculiar demands disappear, or broadly-target competitors address more effectively. It has two variants - cost focus and differentiation focus.

i. Cost Focus

Cost focus seeks cost advantage in the particular segment. While producing products or services, cost is exploited in the optimum level. It uses cost behaviour of the customer segments. An organisation might have several customer segments which can be divided as per price that they willing to pay. Some of the segments can be economically capable of paying more. But a particular segment might be price sensitive and to address this type, the organisation has to produce products or services at a cheaper cost than in the market (Porter, 1985). Also, particular segment might perceive lower price means inferior quality, and to cover this segment, the organisation can add some extraordinary features. Overall, cost focus means controlling or monitoring the cost of production as per specific price concerning the particular segment or group of segment. As the products or services are produced in expected cost and sold in their price, the segment becomes quite happy, and it can be regular to the organisation. As those customers have a close attachment with the organisation, they feel a kind of ownership. Further, in the small market, no other organisation want to adapt cost focus strategy and to attract those customers.

ii. Differentiation Focus

Differentiation focus seeks differentiation advantage in the particular segment or groups of segment. As the market has a particular segment that has unusual needs and desires, and the general products or services can not cover them, this strategy can be applied. Differentiation focus produces the products or services that fulfil their needs and desires. In the beginning, conducting research and providing specific products for a small group might be time-consuming, costly and complicated. But for a long term perspective, the organisation will be rewarded. According to Porter (1985) in such a market, there will not be more competition because new organisations do not dare to enter into this market as it is difficult and risky. Moreover, the market size is too limited, which does not create a big opportunity. In this sense, differentiating in small segments can create competitive advantage. But it is imperative to say that different segments might have their unique or unusual needs to which different technologies, infrastructures, researches and HR skills might be required.

3.2.2. Gray and Balmer's (1998) Corporate Identity

Gary and Balmer's corporate identity indicates to the brand reputation that bestows competitive leverage to an organisation. According to Gray and Balmer (1998), three factors like corporate identity, corporate communication and internal capabilities determine corporate image and reputation of an organisation.

A. Corporate Identity

Corporate identity reflects an organisation's unique characteristics by which its existence is recognised. Every organisation might have their specific features that help customers to create a mental picture of an organisation. Human mind perceive different organisations differently because of their separate identities. For example, Waitrose supermarket represents quality products and higher price whereas Aldi supermarket has a low-quality and lower cost status in the mindset of the customers. So, mostly the higher-class customers buy from Waitrose, and medium or lower-class customers buy from Aldi. These two supermarkets have their different target markets, and they have their identities that have been supporting to attract the target market; thereby, they are achieving competitive advantages. But as the status does not endorse, it cannot survive in the market. Corporate identity is customers' mental picture which remains long-lasting and changing such mindset can be very difficult even after bringing changes in an organisation's attributes (1998).

B. Corporate Communication

Corporate communication indicates overall internal and external sources of communication. An organisation has to communicate its products, services, policies and systems to the related stakeholders. For this purpose, it can use social media, TV, radio, newspaper, booklet, leaflet, website and word of mouth. Means of communication is equally essential aspect of creating a kind of mindset in customers (Gray and Balmer, 1998). In modern business, marketing or communication is critical to develop a positive identity of any business organisation because it adds the value of the products or services. If there is a quality product, but it is not well communicated to the target customers, it cannot increase its sells. Also, its organisation systems and policies should be adequately described with employees, customers, suppliers and other stakeholders. Until and unless there are no effective means of communication, an organisation cannot produce good result.

Corporate image is created through the means of corporate identity and organisational communication. According to Gray and Balmer (1998), in customers' mind, a kind of impression or blueprint appears, which is called corporate image. As the customer identifies needs, then she/he searches product or service options to fulfil the requirements. At that time, corporate image helps in making a buying decision. If the customer has a better corporate image over a particular organisation, such image helps it to sell more products and services. For example, the Coca-Cola Company has a better image in the soft drink beverage industry; thereby, it has been outperforming its competitors. Most of the customers consider it as the synonymous word of cold drink. In short, it has created a positive image among the majority of the customers; thereby, it has been achieving competitive advantage for more than a century. The more an organisation creates a better reputation, the more customers trust over it and become loyal to the brand.

C. Internal Capabilities

An organisation's strong internal capabilities contribute to increase a better chance of achieving competitive advantage in the industry. Internal capabilities are the specific abilities, which are fully controlled or managed by the organisation to achieve strategic aims and objectives. Every organisation wants to increase internal capabilities, but it is not that much easy job.

3.3. Competitive Advantage Components

Competitive advantage is associated with different business components including financial abilities, HRM, supply chain management, product or service quality, technology, infrastructures and marketing (figure 5). An organisation can use one or more than one components, but they must generate extra leverage and help the organisation to outperform the competitors.

A Complete Guide to Ensuring a Successful Business

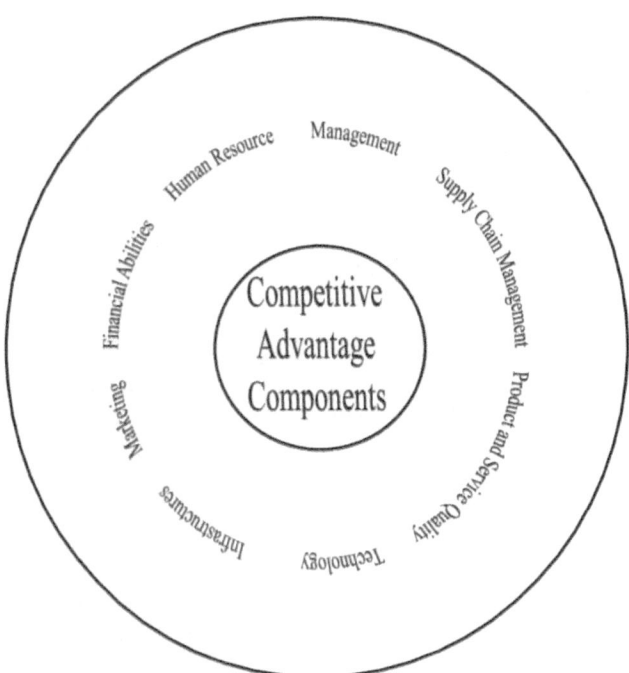

Figure 5: Components of the competitive advantage

3.3.1. Financial Abilities

Finance is an essential factor to operate any business organisation. Broadbent and Cullen (2012) say that financial abilities determine the size of the business, quality of infrastructure, product quality, employees' skills and other aspects. In the lack of finance, these aspects cannot be effectively managed.

3.3.2. Human Resource Management (HRM)

HRM indicates to managing entire human skills and abilities to operate day to day business activities in achieving strategic objectives of an organisation. It includes complete activities related to managing human resources (HR). According to Armstrong (2006), selecting and recruiting the most qualified employees, motivating them to their roles and responsibilities, and enhancing their skills through training and development are the primary tasks of the HRM. It has to ensure the right people in the right position; so, operation would be effective and efficient. It is apparent that if the HRM activities are average, it is difficult to contribute in achieving competitive advantage; they must be perfect or extraordinary.

3.3.3. Supply Chain Management (SCM)

SCM is the entire process of producing products or services. It consists of five key processes such as planning, outsourcing, producing, delivering and gathering customers' feedback (figure 6). This process is associated with producing the most suitable products or services by exploiting the optimum potentiality of the available resources. The essential activity in this process is transforming raw material into the final product. Shah (2009) says that SCM concentrates on producing quality product controlling the cost of production. It outsources quality raw materials, uses of the latest technology, manages employees' talent, cuts unnecessary expense in the overall process, delivers products quickly, reduces stocks as well as raw materials and gives special care in storing.

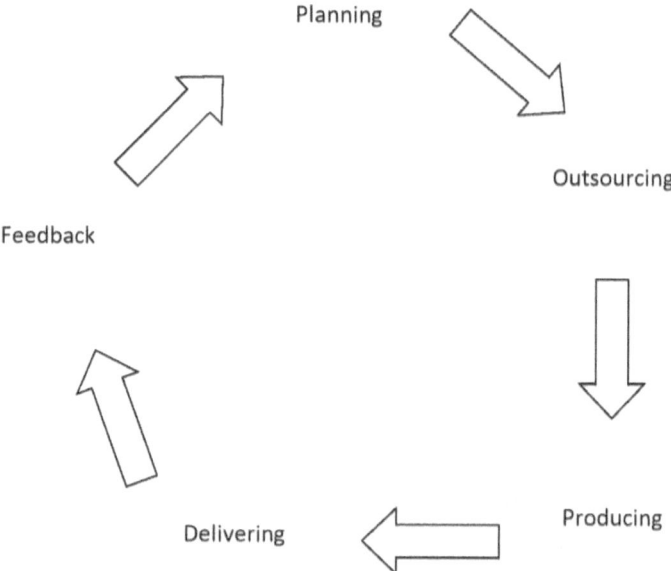

Figure 6: Supply chain management (SCM) process

A. Planning

Planning refers to a detailed preparation or the roadmap of the final destination of the organisation. It evaluates business environment and decides the best procedures. Without a plan, it is difficult to achieve a particular target. It determines what to sell; where to sell; what strategies are going to be applied; who will be the target customers; what are the sources of finance; and many more (Shah, 2009). It helps business organisation to exploit optimum potentiality of the resources.

B. Sourcing

Sourcing indicates to managing the required raw materials and human resources from outside the organisation. Liu (2011) argues that to achieve a competitive advantage, it also plays a vital role because to produce quality products, outsourced raw material and human resource must be extraordinary. As the organisation outsources quality raw materials at a lower cost, it can enjoy a competitive advantage. For example, if Haul restaurant outsources quality raw lamb meat at £3 per kilogram and its competitors outsource same product at £6 per kilogram, the cost of lamb curry at Haul can be lower than its competitors. It can earn more profit if it sells at a competitive price or it can attract more customers if it sells at a lower price. In this regard, outsourcing plays a significant role in allowing competitive benefit to an organisation.

C. Producing

Producing products or services can be the most crucial part of SCM. It is the process of transforming raw material into the finished product. It may involve technologies, HR skills, machines and operations. As this transforming process becomes effective and efficient, the organisation can produce quality products and standard services. SCM exploits resources at the optimum level and produces quality products at a cheaper cost. It indicates that resources have a considerable role in making better products and saving production cost.

D. Delivering

Merely producing products or services cannot be enough to achieve competitive advantage; they must be effectively delivered to the customers. According to Shah (2009), distributing products or services among the customers can be understood as delivering in SMC. There are different means of delivery from displaying at the store to delivering to the customers' door. If a company cannot deliver or provide the product on time, it severely affects brand image. While delivering the products, SCM concentrates over product quality, time, product quantity and locations. Also, in this process, an organisation pays attention to save the original taste of the product by preserving it in the right temperature, using suitable packaging and managing appropriate display.

E. Collecting Feedback

Customers' needs and desires cannot be same all the time; they can be kept on perpetually changing. The product that satisfied customers yesterday may not guarantee to please them today. So, SCM continuously collects customers' feedback to find out the extent to which its products or services have been satisfying customers' needs and desires and what are their further expectations. As per the feedback, it brings necessary improvements on time (Liu, 2011). If an organisation cannot keep customers in its grip, it cannot achieve competitive advantage.

3.3.4. Product and Service Quality

Quality products and services are the primary conditions to satisfy and retain more customers at the organisation. Although producing quality products and services is a complicated job that demands more time, effort and money, it can be rewarded by the premium price which the customers pay happily. Dris and Jain (2007) say that selling low-quality products and services in the market price does not help the organisation to succeed in the market. Even it is sold at a lower price; it cannot achieve competitive advantage because it does not satisfy customers' needs and desires. In the market, there are lots of options; so, even similar quality cannot get any competitive benefit; it must have better quality.

3.3.5. Technology

Technology assists business organisations to perform activities effectively and efficiently. It is a tool or machine that is used to solve the problem(s) in a better way. Today, technology has become an inevitable part of business because, in its absence, production cost will be higher and the quality will be badly affected. It is imperative to say technology has been rapidly changing; so, the old one is replaced by the new one. Along with such changes, the organisations also need to update new technology as quickly as possible. Liu (2011) says that the organisation that uses the latest and most effective technology can produce better quality product and save more cost. Thereby, it can easily outperform its competitors, but if the technology can be easily bought from the market or easily copied, competitive advantage may not sustain for the long term. The technology must be challenging to access or copy by others to maintain such benefit. If a technology is highly costly and the competitors cannot afford it, the competitive advantage can sustain for the long term. Further, if an organisation develops a better technology and the available technologies in the market cannot compete with it, the competitive advantage sustains longer.

3.3.6. Infrastructures

Organisation's facilities such as building, furniture, power supply, instrument and many more can be understood as the infrastructures. According to Sawant (2010), infrastructure does not ensure sustainable competitive advantage because every organisation can easily manage it. They are the essential business components, and if they lack, a business cannot be successful.

3.3.7. Marketing

Marketing indicates to the communication of products and services in the target market. The better target market perceives the products, the higher number of quantity can be sold. If the customers do not know about the brand, the best products also cannot get market. Customers are at the centre of the business; so, they must be aware of new products and services. If the customers know about the products or services, they can try them and continue to use if their needs and desires are better satisfied. Nowadays, a business has to find customers as the customers are passive, and they do not wake up until they are forced to wake up. Only the organisation which becomes able to wake more customers up might be successful in achieving competitive advantage. If there would not be higher competition, the customers would search for products or services, but due to an intense competition, an organisation needs to attract customers. Marketing is the process of introducing new products or reminding the existing products to the target customers (Sullivan and Adcock, 2012). To communicate customers about the products and services, an organisation has to select the right means of communication; choose effective slogan; select the most suitable image, and use catchy message. Besides, it can use different sales promotion tactics such as sample, buy one get one free, price reduction, price pack offer and others. Different tactics might apply to various products and services as per their unique feature. Further, personal selling can also be used in which the seller tries to persuade customers about the benefits of the products and services. If an organisation aggressively uses the marketing strategies, it can create better awareness about the benefits of the products and services; so that, it can sell a higher quantity compared to its competitors.

3.4. The Marketing Mix

Marketing mix indicates to the organisational factors associated with the market. It is an umbrella term that covers significant marketing activities of an organisation. According to Nijssen and Frambach (2001) "marketing mix refers to a coherent set of marketing activities." It clarifies that every systematic activity related to promoting and selling products or services is the marketing mix. The principal purposes of these activities are: to understand market needs; to develop the most suitable products or services; and to sell them in the target market. It forms a positive relationship with customers by satisfying their needs and desires. The more an organisation meets the target customers' expectations the more success it achieves. In this sense, it is not only limited to promotion or selling.

Some people believe that marketing is merely the activities of persuading or informing target customers about products or services to increase sales. But it is very much narrow definition in the sense that it has the responsibility of conducting market research; identifying the most suitable products; determining the most suitable price, and so on. Factors involved in marketing are often understood as the elements of the marketing mix. There are seven elements of the marketing mix, which are called 7Ps of marketing mix. Blythe (2009) says that marketing mix was previously understood as 4Ps (product, price, place and promotion) which was coined by Jerome McCarthy in the 1960s. But in the 1990s other 3Ps (people, process and physical evidence) were added, and now there are 7Ps of marketing mix (figure 7) which has widely being adapted as the theoretical framework of marketing. While developing a business plan, all of these elements must be clearly defined; so that, an organisation can increase its value.

Figure 7: 7Ps of marketing mix

3.4.1. Product

Product is the fundamental factor of a business organisation, which is produced and sold to the customers to fulfil business objectives. It can be any commercial object which can be tangible (goods) or intangible (services). It tries to clarify that products denote both good and service. If there is no product, no business organisation can be imagined; thereby, it can be considered as the heart of the business (Blythe, 2009). Every business organisation has to consider in selecting the right product in the right market.

A market might have several needs and desires which will be challenging to address by a single organisation; thereby, a particular segment(s) should be selected. Further, it is notable to say that a single product may not stimulate customers' attention for long-lasting because it might have a particular life cycle (introduction, growth, maturity and decline). Kumar (2004) says that in different phases, an organisation's roles and responsibilities might be changing. For example, in the maturity phase, its demand will be higher; so that, production ability should be enhanced.

Diversifying product line or increasing its depth might add further value to the product and contribute to increasing number of satisfied customers. For example, in the beginning, Apple Inc. used to produce singe size of iPhone in every version but later on, it identified customers' demands in different sizes of iPhone. So, today, it has been producing the same version in various sizes - iPhone 10 has three options - XS has 5.8", XR has 6.1" and XS Max has 6.5" display (Apple Inc, 2019). All of these models are introduced as the varieties of iPhone X to create stimulation of more customers and cover a broader market segment.

In an organisation, the marketing executive has the key responsibilities in developing the most suitable products. As the product best fulfils customers' needs and desires, it can easily sustain in the market, but as it cannot satisfy them, it disappears from the market. While developing a product, a marketing executive has to consider several factors including target market's needs, product quality, colour, size, product life cycle, price, market competition and many more.

3.4.2. Price

Price is the value that the customers are willing to pay for the particular product. Pricing a product is not an easy job because it is compassionate matter which should consider many factors including production cost, target margin, competition and customers' economic situation. It can have a significant impact on overall marketing strategies because it has a direct relationship with sales and demand. If a firm wants to charge a premium price, the product should be different than its competitors. Better quality product contributes to add value, and the customers can be happy to pay something extra. Customers make a kind of perception about product quality based on the price. If an organisation sells a quality product at a lower price, most of the customers might believe that such product has low-quality. And it creates a negative perception without even a single test. According to Ozer, Ozer and Philips (2012) most of the customers make their buying decision based on the price; so that, they often select the brand that matches their price instead of specific attributes of the particular product. For the compelling pricing, an organisation can apply the most suitable pricing strategies. There are several pricing strategies - market penetration pricing, price skimming, premium pricing, economy pricing, psychological pricing and bundle pricing.

A. Market Penetration Pricing

Market penetration pricing strategy tries to aggressively enter into the market with lower initial price which contributes to attract new customers, increase sales and market share. This kind of strategy can be suitable for new business because it attracts customers to test the product and if they love it; they can be regular. As the product features create a kind of connection between the product and customers, the organisation can slightly increase the price. According to Armstrong, Adam and Denize (2014), this strategy can be equally suitable if there is a higher demand for the product for a short time duration. If its features can be easily copied, it will be sufficiently available in the market very soon. So, before arriving at the competitors' products in the market, this strategy can be used to sell the product in the market aggressively. While selling in the reduced price one has to keep in mind that the firm should have sufficient resources to produce a big quantity of product and every business activity is being operated effectively to save the cost because if the production cost is higher, then this strategy cannot be applicable. Also, lower price assists to stop others from entering into the industry because they do not see profit by selling in such price. This strategy has its advantages and disadvantages which are listed below:

Advantages

- It ensures competitive advantage
- It increases sales, number of customers and share value
- It attracts new customers and satisfies the existing one
- It helps new product or business organisation to establish in the market
- It increases brand image of the organisation

Disadvantages

- If the cost of the product is higher, it is very difficult to generate profit using this pricing strategy
- There is a risk of piling up stock if target sale is not met
- There is a risk of creating low standard brand image in the market
- It will face greater difficulties in increasing price in the future
- As the competitors also use the same strategy, it will create price war, and business cannot earn profit

B. Price Skimming

Price skimming strategy refers to charging a higher price while launching the product, but it reduces later on. As the product is innovative and the competitors can easily imitate it, this pricing strategy can be useful because before the competitors' entry into the market; it allows an organisation to earn maximum profit. Then, it lowers prices to attract price-sensitive customers. Pride and Ferrell (2008) say that by selling at a lower price than the market price, it attracts more customers, increases revenue and increases customer satisfaction level. In the beginning, product will be new in the market, and its demand will not be that much high, but later on, more customers will be aware of it, and the market demand will be increased (figure 8).

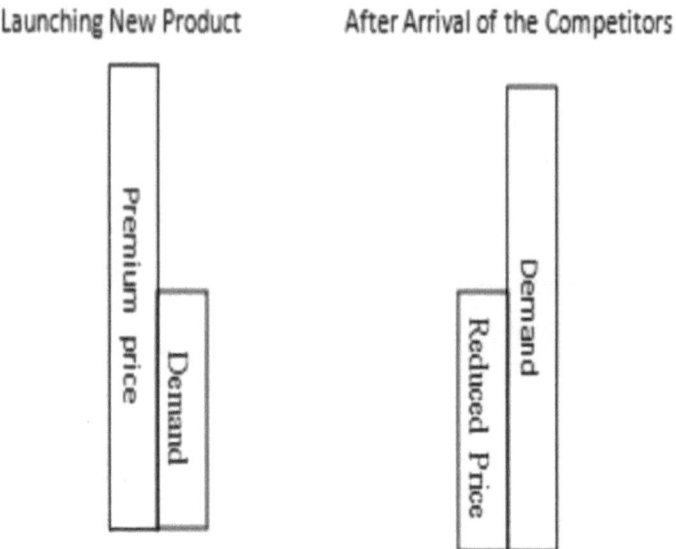

Figure 8: Price-demand relationship in price skimming strategy

This strategy has some advantages and disadvantages which are listed below:

Advantages

- It helps to maximise profitability
- It satisfies more customers and increases share value
- It is flexible; so, it can be adjusted as required
- It helps to target different customer segments (higher, middle and lower class)
- It adds product value

Disadvantages

- Most of the products cannot be sold at a higher price as there are lots of alternative products
- Developing new product can be costly and time-consuming
- If the product does not better fulfil the needs and desires of the customers, this strategy cannot be suitable

- As the price reduces in a short time, the customers who paid premium price might feel to be cheated with phoney price
- If the competitors develop better products, the reduced price may not attract more customers
- In the highly competitive market environment, every competitor is ready to fulfil customers' needs; so, there will not be adequate time to sell product in premium price and maximise profit

C. Premium Pricing

An organisation can sell its unique products at a premium price. Baker (2010) argues that although it is higher than the market price, the customers do not hesitate to pay something extra for the uniqueness. But if an alternative product is available in the market, competitive advantage will not sustain longer, and this pricing strategy also does not work. For example, the iPhone has its unique features in different aspects, from software to design. And such uniqueness has fulfilled customers' needs and desires in a better way, so, it has been charging premium price on its products. An organisation should be able to create premium brand image, and customers should also perceive extra value of the product through different means including product quality, service standard, warranty, packaging, decoration, colour and others to adopt this strategy. It also has some advantages and disadvantages which are listed below:

Advantages

- It contributes to increase profitability of the organisation
- It helps to increase brand awareness and customers' interest in the products
- It is suitable to those organisations which have limited resources

Disadvantages

- It demands costly marketing means of communication that increases an organisation's operational cost

- As the competition increases, there will be a significant challenge in continuing this strategy
- It depends upon limited customers; thereby, small changes in the customers' opinion may lead to a substantial effect in the company's existence
- It requires perpetual innovation of the product which costs much time, effort and money
- This strategy may not be applicable for every business organisation type

D. Economy Pricing

Economy pricing is understood as low margin pricing strategy as it sets a tiny profit. To apply this strategy, a business organisation has to save cost in different sectors including in procurement, energy, stock, human labour, training, marketing and promotion (Sullivan and Adcock, 2012). Only the low-cost production allows an organisation an opportunity to sell product at a lower price. Economic pricing strategy focuses on lower economic class and price-sensitive customers. As the price is lower, an organisation can be able to sell a high volume of products and attract a significant number of customers. If an organisation sells a high quantity, even a tiny profit can also be enough to fulfil its financial objectives. Mostly, this kind of price strategy is applied by the grocery stores. While using this strategy, an organisation should not compromise in quality of the product because if the quality is low, there is no worth of lower price as it cannot attract and retain customers. This strategy has some advantages and disadvantages which are listed as below:

Advantages

- It is useful to attract and retain a significant number of customers
- Organisation can sustain even in the economic recession
- It helps to attract price-sensitive and lower class customers
- It ensures an organisation's competitive leverage

Disadvantages

- It creates a low-quality brand image in the market
- It does not attract higher-class customers
- There is a great possibility to create price war among the competitors
- Smaller businesses which have limited target market cannot apply this strategy
- It does not guarantee customers' loyalty
- Low-cost operation can be difficult to maintain longer

E. Psychological Pricing

Psychological pricing strategy directly affects customers' emotion through an emotional price. Touchy price in attractive tag and design is the major feature of this strategy, which arouses a feeling among the customers that the product is cheaper, and it encourages them to make a buying decision (Pride and Ferrell, 2008). Some of the high street shops are named as 99p shops which indicates that it sells products below £1, and its pricing strategy can be considered as psychological pricing. Instead of pricing £500, some of the organisations' price £499.99 and customers believe that it is cheaper due to psychological effect or left-digit effect. Human mind processes left digit first and compels to act; thereby, this type of pricing strategy tries to find next lower than tens, hundreds and thousands. Such price odd creates a price illusion on customers; that is why the customers believe that the price is lower. Although the difference is tiny, the effect will be massive in making a buying decision, especially in the price-sensitive customers. This strategy came into practice since the early 19th century as the result of price war among different newspapers. Today, it has been established as one of the key pricing strategies in business organisations. It has some advantages and disadvantages which are listed follows:

Advantages

- It increases sales and profitability of the organisation
- It helps to increase the number of customers without a significant discount in price
- -It helps to categorise products based on different cost range like 0-99, 100-199, and so on
- It underpins an organisation to create an affordable brand image

Disadvantages

- Decimal prices make cashier difficult to calculate the amount
- Managing small changes every day might be time-consuming task
- It does not apply to the higher class and rationally guided customers
- It increases customers' doubt in product quality

F. Bundle Pricing

Bundle pricing strategy indicates to selling multiple (two or more than two) products in combined at a lower price than selling them in separately. It helps an organisation to sell overstock because it encourages customers to buy the bundle pack and save money. Rao (2009) argues that this type of pricing strategy contributes an organisation to increase the value of those products which are less popular or have lower demand in the market. It is equally applicable to introduce new product line in the market. The customers get such products at a lower price in bundle, and if they become happy with it, they can be loyal to the brand. This strategy helps customers to save 7% to 15% money compared to buying separately. It has some advantages and disadvantages which are listed as below:

Advantages

- It increases sales volume and revenue of the organisation
- It lowers operational cost and reduces overstock
- It helps to attract new customers and increase share value

- Customers realise greater value of their money
- It assists in marketing new product line
- It underpins to sell the low demand products easily

Disadvantages

- It forces customers to buy unwanted products which might make them unhappy
- Due to unwanted products in the bundle, customers' buying decision might be severely affected
- It reduces an organisation's profitability
- It increases customers' financial burden

3.4.3. Place

Place is the location where the product is stored or displayed to sell. It is a key factor that establishes a connection between product and customers. It is notable to say that the more easily accessible place, the more customers it attracts. Dent and White (2018) say that to determine the most suitable place, a marketing executive must have a deeper insight about the target market and the product attributes. Different products and target markets might require different positioning and distribution channels. There are numbers of distribution channels and out of which physical store, wholesale, direct sales, sales representative and online selling are being highly used in the market.

A. Physical Store

Physical store distribution channel is the physical shop where the customers can directly visit, check the product information and buy it. It is one the most popular distribution channels which can be seen elsewhere in the world (Shareef, Dwivedi and Kumar, 2016). Businesses related to grocery, hospitality, clothing, medicine, education and legal have been using this strategy to sell their products. This distribution channel has some advantages and disadvantages which are listed below:

Advantages

- It allows customers an opportunity to touch, see and feel the product before making a buying decision
- It can be applicable to sell all types of product
- It is the most suitable strategy to target the local customers

Disadvantages

- It is a costly and time-consuming distribution channel
- It has a limited target market
- It is not suitable for those customers who do not have time to visit the physical store

B. Wholesale

Wholesale distribution channel indicates to selling products in a bulk quantity. It mostly targets the retailers instead of the end-users because it does not retail a small amount of product. Dent (2008) states that it plays a significant role between the producers and retailers. Some organisations manufacture themselves, but some others buy from the manufacturing company and sell to the retailers in a bulk quantity. There are some wholesalers like Costco that issues membership and to purchase the products from that store the customers must have a valid membership card. It helps wholesaler to predict sales and to produce the required quantity. It also has some advantages and disadvantages which are listed below:

Advantages

- It creates consistency in sales and profitability
- The retailers' marketing activities facilitate its marketing
- It helps to forecast sales and make effective supply chain management planning
- It does not need to deal with lots of customers

Disadvantage

- It requires a significant amount of capital investment
- It increases inventory cost of the organisation
- Attracting new customers can be a challenging job for it as the customers hardly switch the brand unlike the retail customers

C. Direct Sales

Direct sales uses sales groups who directly reach to the potential customers and persuades them to buy the products. Typically, it uses direct mail, telemarketing or online means of communication. If the product is unique, this kind of distribution channel can be highly useful because it better persuade the target customers by explaining the product features. Both new or existing products can be sold through this channel. According to Launder (2019), it stimulates new customers and increases the brand value of existing products. Also, it helps to establish new product in the market. It also has some advantage and disadvantages which are listed below:

Advantages

- It creates the company's direct relationship with customers
- It helps to increase the profitability of the company
- It will have better control over marketing strategies
- It is highly applicable for selling unique products

Disadvantages

- It is not suitable to sell general products and to target a large market
- It weakens the organisation's focus by dividing into two functions - production and distribution
- It requires marketing experts who are not easy to be recruited
- It will be costly, time-consuming but less effective

D. Sales Representative

Sales representative distribution channel refers to selling the products by deploying the company's sales staffs. It is similar to the direct sales in the sense that a company directly involves in distributing or selling process. To promote the product, the sales staffs visit customers, participate in trade show or exhibition and conduct presentation. Mostly, they visit target customers face to face, but sometimes they can use email, social media, call or text message. According to Careers (2018), unlike in direct sales, it recruits marketing staffs as the sales representatives and their responsibilities will be persuading customers to buy the products. It has some advantages and disadvantages which are listed below:

Advantage

- It increases sales and revenue of the organisation
- It is useful to sell unique or new products
- It contributes to understand market needs and desires effectively
- It helps to increase customer loyalty
- It allows customers an opportunity to know products' detail

Disadvantages

- It increases HRM cost
- It is not useful to sell a large quantity of product
- It is not appropriate to sell general and cheaper products

E. Online Selling

Online selling does not have its physical store; it displays images of the product and gives necessary information, including product description, price, delivery, and terms and conditions through online means. It is a form of electronic commerce in which a company sells products without directly visiting the customers. As the customers buy the products through the internet, the company delivers the products at the customers' door. Some of the companies provide the delivery service free of charge, but some others have a reasonable fee. Through the means of this channel, all type of product from grocery products to valuable ornaments can be sold.

According to Hofacker (2019) nowadays, it has been popular in the market along with increasing customers' accessibility in internet, computer and Smartphone. Today, customers surf the products on the internet, compare with alternative products and make a buying decision. They do on want to visit physical store and waste time, effort and travel cost. This distribution channel can be equally suitable for business to business (B2B) as well as business to customers (B2C) sales. It has some advantages and disadvantage which are listed below:

Advantages

- It can cover a broader target market
- It is a cost-effective means of distribution channel
- In this channel, the customers can easily and quickly find the product
- It saves customers' time, money and effort
- It can be equally applied in B2B and B2C businesses

Disadvantages

- The customers cannot have an opportunity to touch, see, feel, smell or taste the products directly before making a buying decision
- The delivery cost might increase the operational cost of the organisation
- Sometimes, customers might need to wait for a long time to get the product to be delivered
- If the customers do not like the product after receiving, they may need to pay posting/delivery charges

3.4.4. Promotion

Promotion is the process of making the target market aware of the products. In the modern business, promotion can be recognised as one of the imperative components of marketing because it directly or indirectly communicates to the target customers to increase brand image and sales. The more effective promotion, the better an organisation sells its products. If there is no promotion, the customers do not know about the products; thereby, the organisation cannot sell them even they are better than the products available in the market. It is comprised of different elements like sales promotion, advertising, personal selling, direct marketing and public relation, which are collectively understood as promotional mix (figure 9).

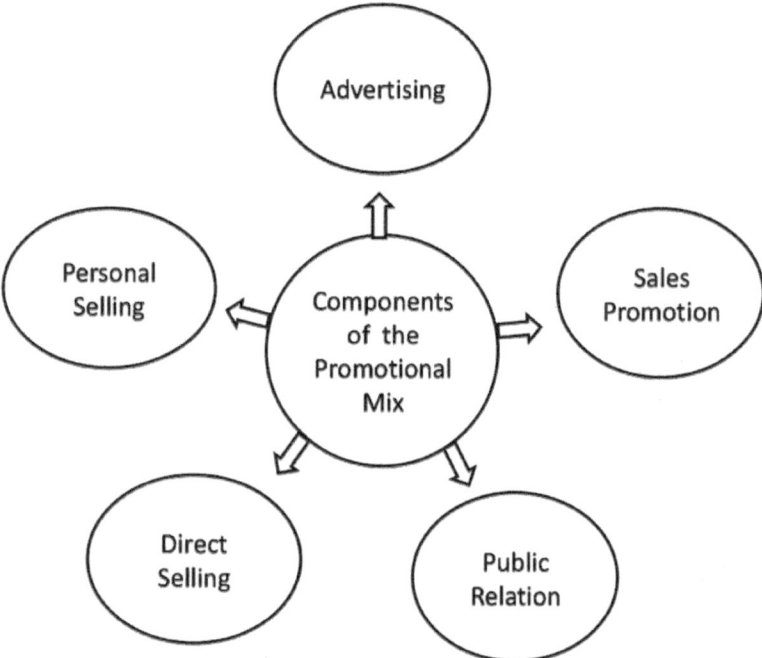

Figure 9: Components of the promotional mix

A. Sales Promotion

Sales promotion is one of the variants of promotional mix that creates urgency to buy the products and services. Although it is a short term incentive, it contributes an organisation to maintain a long term customer relationship. Groucutt (2005) says that it is used to promote new product, attract customers in the existing product, increase overall sales and reduce stock. According to Etzel (2007), "Sales promotion is sponsor-funded, demand stimulating activity designed to supplement advertising and facilitate personal selling. It frequently consists of temporary incentives to encourage a sale or purchase." This definition clarifies that it facilitates personal selling and becomes supplement of the advertising. Kotler and Armstrong (2008) say that it is a short term incentive that encourages customers to involve in buying activities. They insist that advertising focuses on reason to buy but sales promotion on emotion to buy. Perreault and McCarthy (2006) try to separate sales promotion from advertising, personal selling and publicity and view as the purchase stimuli. Hoffman (2005) says that manufacturers use it to introduce a new product or promote the existing product, whereas retailers use to stimulate customers and increase sales.

A firm uses sales promotion tactic to reinforce the existing product; switch the brand; improve customer relationship; reduce overstock, and increase revenue. Pride et al. (2011) state that sales promotion activities have direct inducement with customers. It tries to maintain consistency between the organisational goals and the marketing/promotional goals. Further, it is used to enhance other promotional methods. Pride et al. (2011) have identified ten objectives of sales promotion tactic, and they are:

1. To attract new customers
2. To encourage customers for new product trial
3. To invigorate the sales of mature brand
4. To boost sales by aggressive selling
5. To reinforce advertising
6. To increase traffic in retail store

7. To steady the irregular sales pattern
8. To build up resellers' inventories
9. To naturalise competitive promotional effect
10. To improve shelf space and display

Similarly, Lee and Johnson (2005) say that sales promotion can appeal the customers to achieve a firm's various marketing objectives by:

1. Introducing new product
2. Inducing current customers to buy more products
3. Maintaining sales in off-seasons
4. Obtaining greater shelf-space
5. Combating the competition

Sales promotion can employ various tools which can be determined based on the nature of a firm and its objectives. Pride et al. (2011) say that most of the promotional tools can be classified into two categories: consumer sales and trade sales.

Consumer sales promotion is the marketing tool that is used to entice the customers to buy as much as possible. It is applied for a short period to increase market share or introduce new product in the market. The consumer sales promotion includes different tools like sampling, free trial, gift, contests, and special pricing (Joseph, 2013). But trade sales promotion is used by a manufacturing company or the wholesalers to encourage resellers or retailers to sell more products. It includes tools like trade allowances, co-operative advertising and dealer listing, free merchandise and gifts, and premium money (Hoffman et al., 2005). There are numbers of sales promotion techniques which are briefly discussed below:

i. Price Cut/Sale Offer

The price cut or sales offer stimulates demand for the short term (Smith, 2011). This tool allows customers an opportunity to get product at a discounted price through different means like half price, save 1/3, better than half price and buy one get one free.

ii. Discount Voucher/ Coupon

Greer (2010) defines voucher as a redeemable discount or offer, which is distributed by the organisation to the customers. It might have certain conditions like valid for specific products, particular time, minimum purchase amount, and others. Frasel and Druce (2006) say that coupon entices customers to buy the products within the limited time frame. To be benefited by the offer, the customers purchase the product even they do not need that item immediately. It can be distributed by using various channels like online, text message, in-store display shelf, and others. Kotler and Armstrong (2008) argue that coupon or discount voucher can be suitable to introduce new products or sell less popular products.

iii. Disguised Price Cut

Disguised price cut sales promotion is one of the best tools that helps an organisation to maintain a regular price structure by offering customers some incentives. Middleton and Clarke (2012) say that it gives a discount or offer in one product and through other products, it maintains cost. For example, a hotel can offer a double bedroom in the price of a single bedroom, but it adds the value or earns profits through other products like meal, bar and transportation. So, at the surface level, it seems to be an offer, but the business maintains its balance price and profit through other products.

iv. Extra Product

Extra product sales promotion indicates to providing an additional product without an extra charge (Gupta and Randhawa, 2008). Offers like buy two and get one free or buy a computer and get free window software are some of the examples of this type of sales promotion. Here, the main product adds value, whereas an offer products entice customers.

v. Additional Service

Additional service is another essential incentive that is used by an organisation to attract more customers. A retailer can provide an additional facility free of cost. Some of the organisations offer free delivery services over a certain amount of purchase. Some car retailers offer free servicing for two years. Based on the nature of an organisation, it can be different from one organisation to another. Those additional services are offered for a limited time; that is why, the customers feel urgency to grab the opportunity (Groucutte, 2005).

vi. Free Gift

Gift is a separate product that is provided by an organisation to the customers as they purchase a particular product (Trehan and Trehan, 2007). For example, an organisation can give pen, diary and others as the gift. It can be equally used by the manufacturers or wholesalers to motivate retailers for selling more products. To encourage the retailer "a company may give gift like watches, clocks or transistor radios to the dealers based on the volume of order placed. It may serve as a useful reminder of the dealer's link to the company." (Mohan, 1989) Gift incentives build a close relationship between the dealer and the company. The more a company has a close relationship with dealers, the more she/he will be motivated in selling more products.

vii. Competition

Competition sales promotion tool can be used to attract customers and retailers. It is an interest-based sales promotion, which is related to either money or value. Sullivan and Adcock (2012) say, "Competitions give shopper something for nothing and can provide an air of excitement." It is designed to create an interest by offering money or value.

viii. Passport Scheme

Murthy and Bhojanna (2007) define passport scheme as something exciting gift that is given to the existing customers. It is designed to reward and promote loyalty of the customers and frequency in the purchases.

ix. Prize Draw

Prize draw is identical to the lottery, but there is no entry free. Further, entry does not tie with the purchase qualification, which means to say that every customer is equally eligible to get entry in the prize draw. According to Thomas (1995), it is a fair and reliable tool in which everyone has an equal chance to win the prize. It can be used as a customer sales promotion tool as well as a distribution network. Loton (2008) says that no rule guides prize draw; the winners are randomly selected that provides an equal opportunity for every participant.

x. Extra Commission

An industry encourages its dealer/distribution networks by offing an extra commission. Beaver (2005) says that additional commission is paid to motivate the sales outlet to sell more product. For example, if the dealer meets a particular target, it gets extra benefit that entices to sell further products of the brand.

xi. Parties

A producer, sometimes, gives a party for its retailers to increase a kind of intimacy with them (Silverberg and Cullen, 2006). It attracts retailers' attention to the product, and she/he tries to sell more products of the brand.

xii. Bonuses

Yeshin (2006) says that bonus is one of the highly accepted sales promotion tactics, which contributes to boost the sales in overnight. It is provided based on the retailers' performance; so, it encourages to sell more product of the particular supplier.

xiii. Travel Incentives

Travel incentive is also one of the popular means of sales promotion that allows certain destination travel based on the retailers' sales performance.

The more a dealer sales product, the better travel incentive it receives (Dibb and Simkin, 2012).

B. Advertising

Advertising indicates to a non-personal message that is conveyed to the target market, aiming to aware customers about the product features. It can be used to introduce new products or new features of existing products or to reinforce existing products. It focuses on reasons to buy the product; so, it highlights positive features, including brand value, product quality, price, delivery, services, design and many more. The modern form of advertising began along with tobacco advertising in the 1920s. Since that, its application has been perpetually increasing, and billions of dollars have been globally spent on it (figure 10).

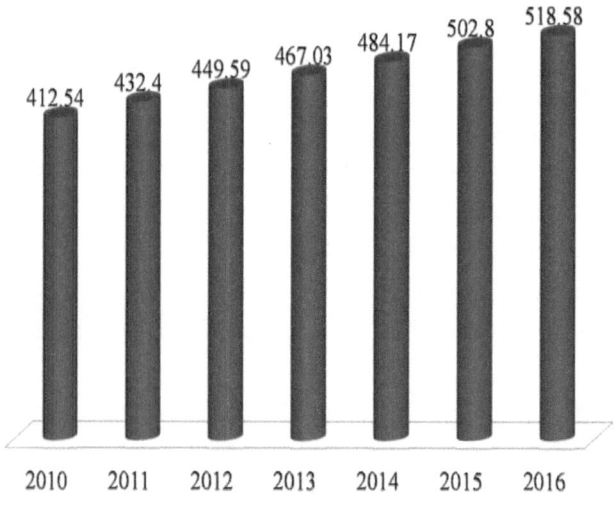

Figure 10: Globally spent amount in advertising (in billion US dollar) (Source: Statista, 2019)

The above figure clarifies the extent to which money is spent in advertising. Currently, business is impossible without effective advertising. There are different tools of advertising, which can be broadly divided into two types: traditional and modern means of communication.

i. Traditional Means of Communication

All of the communication media that were available before the introduction of the internet and mobile phone are considered as the traditional means of communication, and they are newspapers, magazine, radio, TV, post and hooding board. Out of these media, TV has the most powerful impact on customers because it uses sound, word and visual that helps to convey the message effectively (Varey (2002). It helps an organisation to persuade customers and affect their buying decision. But as the drawbacks, its message cannot be saved or watched whenever and wherever it is required. At the same time, it can make people annoyed if any unwanted advertising keeps on coming while watching a favourite program. And it is an expensive means of advertising that increases the operational cost of an organisation.

Regarding radio, the customers cannot have an opportunity to view the products and read the script; it uses only sound to convey the message. This type of media advertisement is cheaper compared to TV advertising. But radio advertising is not as effective as TV advertising. Like TV advertising, this type of advertising also cannot be saved and listened as per required.

Newspaper, magazine and post advertisements do not use voice; they use only script and picture. This type of advertising can be saved to read information in future as it is required. For example, when a cab company posts a business card to the target customer's door, it can be saved in the wallet or somewhere else, and the customer can use the contact details whenever it is required.

Regarding hooding board, information can be displayed to a particular location that helps to remind a big market.

ii. Modern Means of Communication

Modern means of communication like website, phone call, text message, email, social media and online advertising blog/site are popular at present.

Internet-based media are called digital media which is highly prevalent in business organisations. According to Handley (2017) by 2020, half of the advertising amount will be spent on online media. It tries to clarify that the use of modern means of communication has been significantly increasing. Online media advertisement uses visual, script and sound to persuade and attract potential customers. This kind of advertising can be retrieved at any time and from anywhere. For example, the customers can check product information on the company's website from elsewhere in the world and anytime using the internet. Unlike TV advertisement, the pictures can be enlarged and read or listen the information repeatedly. At the same time, by using the internet, customers can contact the organisation if they have any queries. Regarding e-commerce, products can be ordered through the website or online e-commerce sites.

Email and text messages use only script whereas phone call uses voice. They can convey the message directly to the potential customers, but collecting the potential customers' email address or contact number might be a difficult job. If they are directly contacted, there will be a high possibility of increasing sales. For example, business organisations collect their customers' emails or phone numbers, and then they convey the message directly. If the customers do not want to receive such marketing messages, they can unsubscribe their email or ask to stop contacting or messaging again.

C. Public Relation

Public relation (PR) is the process of creating a mutual relationship between an organisation and the public based on the mutual benefit. In other words, it is a communication between an organisation and the public. This type of communication has significant differences with advertising in the sense that its exposure or publicity is related to the public interest instead of any direct selling purpose. It contributes customers to develop a positive perception of the organisation, which increases customers' loyalty. Spacey (2017) says that the primary aim of the PR is to inform stakeholders about the products and gain their support. Most of the renowned companies recruit the PR executive or the manager to develop a positive public influence to the organisation. Their key responsibilities will be designing communication campaign, conducting conference, writing news and articles, participating in media interview, meeting with public, participating in public programs, and preparing social media contents. To create a good PR, the PR manager must understand the concerns of the stakeholders and address them effectively. For example, if the local public produce vegetables in their field and they are looking for the market, a grocery shop should give space for those products. According to Spacey (2017), there are different types of PR - media relation, investor relation, government relation, community relation, internal communication, customer relation and marketing communication (figure 11).

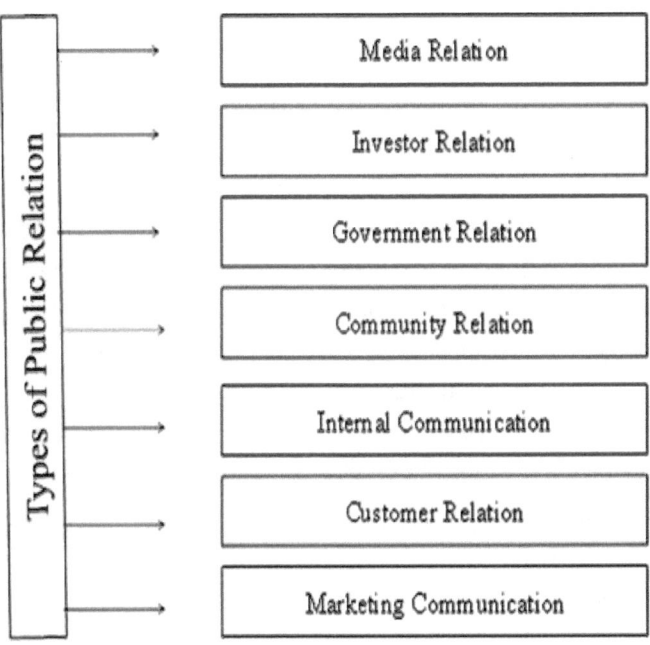

Figure 11: Types of Public Relation

i. Media Relation

An organisation can make a public relations and create a brand reputation through the means of news or article. Media relation has an indirect relationship with sales of products because it does not directly appeal to customers to buy the products. But by increasing corporate reputation, it indirectly helps to attract and retain the customers. Johnston (2013) says that based on the media news, the general public make an opinion about the brand or organisation. So that, it plays a significant role to succeed an organisation in fulfilling its strategic aims and objectives.

ii. Investor Relation

Relationship between a business organisation and its investors or potential investors is the investor relation. To maintain this type of relationship, an organisation has to fulfil different responsibilities: organising investors' seminar, preparing financial report, responding queries of various stakeholders and releasing press news. The investors want to increase the retained earnings or share value of the investment to which they want to know business strategies, objectives, target market and many more (Ryan and Jacobs, 2005). All of these aspects can be addressed in the financial report, but in case of start-up business, they can be included in the business plan. An organisation has to make its investors and potential investors aware of the investment opportunities. As the interest is aroused, they read the business plan or financial report for further information. It is essential to say that investor relationship does not only mean to attract new investors; it is equally the process of communicating with existing investors. If the existing investors are not satisfied, the organisation finds difficulties in sustaining its value. The more an organisation maintains a positive relationship with investors, the better brand loyalty can be created in the market.

iii. Government Relation

An organisation operates its business activities under particular business laws and regulations of the state. The government has numbers of concerns including fair competition, health and safety at workplace, consumer rights, environment save and employment (Gregory, 2004). The government can have concerns over these issues, and every organisation has to address those concerns. To understand governments' position about those issues, PR plays a significant role. An organisation has to keep the government in confidence, ensuring that the organisation has been following governments' rules and regulations while operating its business activities.

iv. Community Relation

Every organisation has to build a positive relationship with the local community to get constructive support in fulfilling strategic objectives. A negative relationship perishes organisation's image and decreases share value; thereby, it is essential to create a positive community relation. Gregory (2004) says that every community wants an organisation's positive contributions in different social issues including saving environment, quality life, employment, sales of local products, peace, community awareness program and safety. As an organisation pays attention to these aspects, there will be a good relationship between the organisation and the community.

v. Internal Communication

Internal communication indicates a communication with the employees about business objectives, strategies and cultures. An organisation can manage employees' meeting to educate them about the details of the organisation, which is also a task of PR. If there is no internal communication, it is challenging to develop a positive relationship with the public.

vi. Customer Relation

Customers are the key stakeholders of a business organisation as they determine its success or failure. According to Jha (2008), if an organisation does not have a good relationship with customers, it cannot satisfy their needs and desires. The more an organisation has a close relationship with customers, the better it can increase its sales by attracting new customers and retaining the existing one. Better customer relationship allows organisation an opportunity to integrate with customers' feelings and expectations.

vii. Marketing Communication

Marketing communication indicates the process of conveying a message to the target market, aiming to stimulate demand through brand awareness. In can be used to introduce the new products as well as to reinforce existing products. The message can be delivered through different tools like advertising, sales promotion, direct marketing and personal selling (Egan, 2007). It is the process of approaching a brand to the target market. In this competitive market environment, it is impossible to fulfil business objective without an effective marketing communication.

D. Direct Marketing

Direct marketing is one of the vital promotional approaches in which an organisation directly conveys its message to the target customers. Unlike advertising, it focuses on a small target market or the potential customers. Since it is more direct to the prospective customers, it is called direct marketing. The primary purpose of this marketing is to persuade customers to make a buying decision. It is imperative to say that everyone may not be equally ready to buy the products on the spot. But at least they visit the website, contact organisation for further information and remind the brand.

Direct marketing focuses on those customers who are likely to be the buyers. Moreover, as the personal message is sent, potential customers may feel that they have got special attention, which helps them to realise a kind of closeness with the brand. Also, as it is only targeted to potential customers, it saves a tremendous cost of marketing in the broader and less effective market. Further, the progress can be highly measurable because each campaign's progress can easily be tracked. There are different forms of direct marketing which are: brochure, catalogue, phone call, text message, email, flier, post, coupon and targeted online displayed ad (figure 12).

Figure 12: Different forms of direct marketing

i. Brochure

Brochure is an informative paper which can be folded in the shape of pamphlet or leaflet and distributed to the target customers. Mullin (2002) says that it covers many features of the product as its size is relatively larger. It can be used to introduce a brand or inform about products to the prospective customers. It is distributed through different means like post, email, newspaper and direct distribution.

ii. Catalogue

Catalogue is a list of the products and their features. Unlike brochure, it has several pages; so that, sometimes, it looks like a book. It can be online as well as paper-based, but online one can be more effective because it can be easily accessed by the broader range of target customers (Roberts and Berger, 1999). Further, online brochure can be cost-effective, and it immediately reaches to the target customers across the world.

iii. Phone Call

An organisation can directly make a call to the customers and give information about the products. It contributes an organisation to understand customers' needs and encourage them in making a buying decision. For example, some of the mobile phone companies make a direct call to persuade customers to buy the products and services. Roberts and Berger (1999) say that although phone call is a necessary means of direct marketing, most of the times, it makes customers annoy because such calls may disturb them. If they are interested, it is all right; otherwise, they feel it is a waste of time, and it increases their dissatisfaction. Further, getting phone numbers of the target customers can also be a difficult job.

iv. Text Message

It is a short written message that is sent to the potential customers' mobile phone number. It reaches to a large number of customers in one click. Also, it does not disturb as much as the phone call because the customers do not need to take immediate action over the text (Haig, 2002). They can ignore it if they are not interested, but if they are interested, they can follow the information and make purchases. But collecting the contact numbers of the target customers is a challenging job associated with this type of marketing tool.

v. Email

Email is one of the crucial direct marketing tools, which is used to send information via the internet to the target customers' email account. Mullen and Daniels (2011) say that it is a quicker, effective and efficient means of marketing because it can be sent to a vast number of customers in a single click which reaches accounts immediately across the world.

There is no worry of missing information because it can be accessed anytime and from anywhere. But, same as phone call, collecting contact detail (emails) can be difficult.

vi. Flier

Flyer is typically single-sided paper that contains bold and colourful words with a clear message. It is a concise form of advertisement that informs and attracts potential customers, unlike brochures. It includes some attractive figures, slogans and significant features of the brand or product. It is a single page advertising, but page size can be different as per required. And it can be handed over to the potential customers or posted to their home addresses.

vii. Post

An organisation can make direct communication with target customers through the postal mail. Message can be posted as the form of letter, and the authorised or targeted person opens it. Due to the nature of specific marketing, the customers take it seriously than general advertising. Return on investment of this means of promotion is higher, and it can be the most suitable to focus on short distance target market. And compared to other tools, it is supposed to be more authentic, official and reliable. It better persuades customers about products or brand. But if the target market is in far distance, the postage charge will be higher and delivery time will also be longer. Also, it does not ensure whether the authorised person will open the post or not.

viii. Coupon

Coupon is company's financial discount or rebate offer, which can be found either in paper and online form. Smith and Taylor (2004) say that coupon is like a cheque which can be used to get discount while purchasing certain products or services. It is considered as one of the critical sales promotion tactics because it encourages customers to make a buying decision as soon as possible. Further, it helps to increase revenue and customer satisfaction. Also, it underpins to reduce overstock, introduce new products and sell low popular products. It can be distributed through store, post, email, newspaper, social media and high street. It helps customers to save at least some money; thereby, they make buying decision before the expiry date of the coupon. Some of the customers buy products to use coupon, although that product is not required for immediate use. They are not certain whether they can get such offer in future or not; that is the reason, they make a quick buying decision.

ix. Targeted Online Displayed ad

Targeted online displayed ad is different than online advertising because it targets only particular customers instead of customers in general. It can be used as a banner ad or advanced form of video for the specific program (Jones, 2009). For example, in a migraine-related video program, banner of Vanquish pain-killer advertising can be displayed. This type of video is often watched by the people who have this problem or have someone or have a keen interest in it. So, the Vanquish advertising in such program can be useful to persuade customers.

E. Personal Selling

Personal selling indicates to making sales through the mean of salespersons who are recruited by the company to meet customers directly and sell the products. They have specific knowledge about the products and better communication skills; so that, they can persuade customers to buy the products. Also, they can demonstrate the application of the product if it is required. Ingram, LaForge and Avila (2012) say that when the customers are convinced about the benefits of products, either they buy it or make a trial to see how it fulfils their needs and desires. Some of the cosmetic products and luxury products which have a relatively high price or exceptional feature are usually sold using this type of promotion. Mostly the perfumes are being sold in high street by the salespersons. It does not mean that it is not relevant to sell other types of products, but its effectiveness may not be that much.

Personal selling can be highly useful for selling products to the retailers (Agarwal, 1982). The salespersons directly meet retailers, persuade them to order a bulk quantity and encourage them to put the products in the primary location of the store. Sales promotion lures retailers to sell more products of a particular brand. Also, the personal selling allows organisation an opportunity to understand the needs and desires of the retailers and to develop the most suitable strategies. It has some advantages and disadvantages which are listed below:

Advantages

- Salesperson can meet customers directly and communicate face to face
- Use of gesture, emotion and facial expression make the communication more persuasive
- Customers' feelings and attitudes about the products can be understood
- Customers' attention can be more considerable in face to face communication
- It provides customised message which will be more effective
- Customers get a close interaction opportunity about the products
- It has an excellent opportunity to close the sales
- It helps to increase the positive relationship between the brand and the customers
- Customers' feedback can be easily collected to improve the product quality
- This promotion will be highly productive for the manufacturing companies to sell their products to retailers

Disadvantages

- Due to the customised message, it incurs higher marketing cost

- It requires highly trained and motivated sales representatives
- It cannot be suitable for a broader target market
- It may not be applicable to sell low price or ordinary product
- It might face significant problems in meeting target customers

Types of Personal Selling

Based on the buyers, personal selling can be divided into three types: retail selling, business-to-business selling, and trade selling.

i. Retail Selling

Retail selling indicates to selling products or services to the customers in a small quantity. Here, the buyers are the customers who buy for their use or consumption. According to Sullivan and Adcock (2012), the salesperson visits customers at their doors or any other convenient place and covey the customised message that helps them to understand the product features. This type of selling is more useful to sell the unique, expensive and new products. But, visiting individual customer at her/his location is costly and time-consuming marketing process. Further, it requires enthusiastic, self-motivated and trained salesperson.

ii. Business-to-Business (B2B) Selling

Business-to-business personal selling refers to selling the products to the industrial buyers. The salesperson visits different industries to sell the products. For example, the salespersons of a cow farm might visit a dairy factory to sell the milk. As it has B2B relation, the sales quantity and the return on investment will be higher. Further, it helps an organisation to maintain a good relationship with its buyers, understand their needs, collect feedback on the products and increase revenue (Zimmerman and Blythe, 2017). In this type of personal selling, the salesperson must be highly motivated, knowledgeable, skilful and persuasive. But to manage or recruit such HR, an organisation might cost much time, effort and money.

iii. Trade Selling

Unlike B2B selling, the marketing intermediaries like retailers and wholesalers will be the buyers of the trade selling. The salespersons directly visit to those intermediaries and encourage them to buy the products, who purchase a bulk quantity of product and sell to the customers or end-users (Kurtz and Boone, 2008). Most of the organisations use this type of personal selling to sell their products. For example, a salesperson visits hospital, medical centre and pharmacies to persuade them to buy her/his medicine. Sometimes, she/he offers sales promotion that makes retailers easy to make immediate buying decision. It is imperative to mention that the return on investment of this type of personal selling is higher because it dramatically increases the revenue. Also, the salesperson can have an opportunity to meet the manager of the retail or wholesale company directly, organise presentation, maintain a close relationship with the organisation, understand their needs and encourage them to make a buying decision. As they are convinced, the organisation can receive a bulk quantity of order. But this type of personal selling cannot be applicable to sell a small amount of product. Similarly, to persuade the intermediaries, the salesperson must be highly qualified, professional, knowledgeable, self-motivated and persuasive. But to recruit or develop such skills, an organisation might cost more time, effort and money.

3.4.5. People

People is one of the key marketing mix elements. Here, the term people indicates to the employees who are directly or indirectly working in different sectors of an organisation like production, service, and marketing and distribution (Lamb, Hair and McDaniel, 2008). In other words, everyone whose activities are related to producing and selling products can be understood as people. If there are no people, an organisation cannot operate its business activities, and no marketing mix can be in complete form. People are the heart of any business organisation. Every event like market research, product design, manufacturing, display, marketing, communication and delivery can be only possible through this marketing mix. People have

Dr Yubraj Giri

numbers of roles which can be studied by dividing into seven key sectors: production, customer service, public relation, management, research and development, finance and marketing (figure 13).

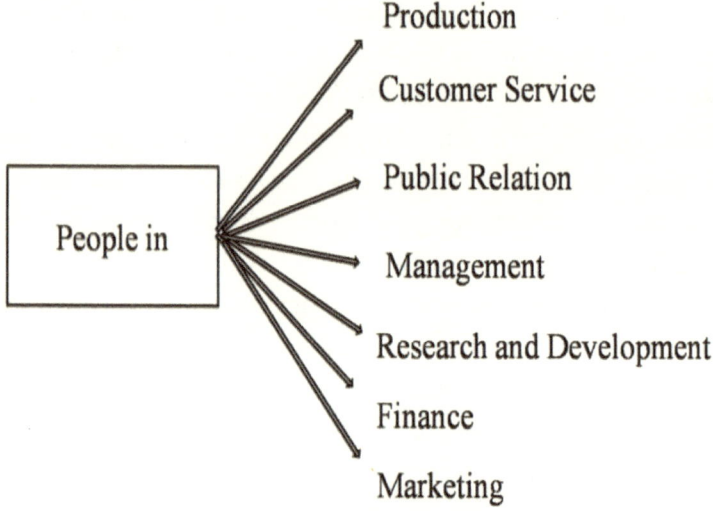

Figure 13: People's role in different sectors

A. People in Production Sector

Some of the employees might have their job responsibilities in the production sector, and their role is to produce quality products efficiently and effectively. If there are right people in the right place, their performance underpins in fulfilling strategic objectives of the organisation. Considering the fact, while recruiting people in the production sector, an organisation has to give much more focus on selecting the most suitable candidate(s). As the product contributes to making a brand image of an organisation, people in production section must be qualified, expert, trained and highly deserving.

B. People in Customer Service Sector

Customer service indicates to offering the required assistance to the customers by an organisation. The employees who are responsible for assisting customers before, in the course of buying and after buying the products are called customer service executives who have a direct relationship with customers. There might be numbers of responsibilities of customer service executives such as: describing product features, making transaction, returning products, serving the purchased products, resolving customers' queries, finding out the best options and making them familiar in the organisation's system (Cook, 2004).

C. People in Public Relation Sector

Some of the organisations recruit employees to make an excellent public relation with customers. Here, the public refers to everyone who is directly or indirectly associated with the organisation. Theaker (2004) says that local organisations, government, customers, employees and investors can be the public. Different public sectors might have different expectations which should be understood by the public relation executives and try to address them effectively. For example, Sainsbury's Supermarket contributed to the local schools through Nectar Points in which it became successful in engaging customers. As the customers earned points, they could donate it to the local schools and Sainsbury's would double the points. The schools could redeem those points while buying school stationeries. In the local public, it created a positive impact, and they considered the organisation as a significant part of the local community.

D. People in Management Sector

The people who plan, execute and monitor the activities of an organisation are known as the management body. They are responsible for communicating the business plan to the related stakeholders, manage human resources, arrange infrastructure, manage financial resources, and many more. According to Smith, Thorpe and Jackson (2015), if the management is not practical, business performance cannot adequately explore the optimum potentiality of the resources; thereby, every organisation pays serious attention while recruiting the managerial staffs. In the management team, the manager will have a significant responsibility, and her/his management abilities determine the effectiveness of the entire administrative team. The manager should have numbers of skills including decision making, risk-taking, persuasive, patience, foresightedness, and many more to manage an organisation effectively.

E. People in Research and Development (R&D) Sector

Most of the giant companies recruit research and development professionals who research on developing compelling products and satisfying the needs and desires of the target customers. In the competitive market environment, customers' needs and wants are rapidly changing and to address such changes, R&D professionals develop innovative products and services (Laws, 2003). It is imperative to say that small organisations may not be able to afford these professionals, and the impacts will also not be significant. As per the required, an organisation can decide whether to recruit such professionals or not. For example, in the medical sector, a pharmaceutical company's highest spending will be in the R&D sector. Such organisations entirely depend upon the R&D; the more it produces innovative products, the better the organisation achieves competitive advantages.

F. People in Financial Sector

Most of the larger companies might have substantial financial transaction; so, it is difficult for them to record and manage without recruiting accountant(s) or financial adviser(s) unlike in the small companies. Accountants record various transactions, including revenue, cost, interest, tax, loan and others. Also based on the transaction, they prepare an annual business report. They record every penny in their financial statement, which makes easy to assess the financial performance of an organisation. In the same way, financial advisors suggest organisation the most suitable financial resources, money management strategy, cost-saving techniques, insurance policy, tax law, methods of achieving long term financial goals and others (Carmichael and Graham, 2012).

G. People in Marketing Sector

Marketing is related to fulfilling the strategic objectives of an organisation through the means of selling products to the target customers. Although some people believe that it is merely the process of selling products, but it is not limited to such a small role (Chikuhwa, 2013). It is related to conducting market research, designing suitable products, promoting the products and collecting customers' feedback. Marketing employees have a vital role in creating a positive brand image by promoting specific attributes of the products. In a small business, there may not be separate marketing employees, but the marketing activities will be there, and the management team can execute those activities.

3.4.6. Process

Process refers to a system of producing desirable products by transforming inputs or resources. It has three key stages - input, throughput and output. There is an essential role of marketing activities to make the process effective because they provide a valuable intelligence of the market to produce the most suitable products. According to Blythe (2009) process is a system that determines how the activities should be performed to achieve the target objectives. There are different types of processes which can be studied under two segments: direct and indirect.

A. Direct Marketing Related Process

Direct marketing related process has five-step procedures: setting marketing objectives process, market targeting process, market research process, communication process and market growth process, which are described as below:

i. Setting Marketing Objectives Process

An objective governs every marketing activity; thereby, setting a realistic and achievable goal is an important task. To develop a practical purpose, the marketing team can follow the following processes:

- Understand the target market
- Collect information about the product
- Evaluate internal and external business environmental factors
- Formulate SMART objectives
- Receive feedback and make necessary improvements

ii. Market Targeting Process

Market is an umbrella term that includes a broader range of customers who might be located in different geographical locations; different interest; be from different classes; and so on. An organisation might not cover or target the entire market; in this sense, it has to select the most suitable segment(s). To target the most favourable segment(s), an organisation can follow the following processes:

- Divide the market into different segments based on the business nature
- Identify the most suitable categories (geographical, class, religion, age, interest and others)
- Understand the attributes of different segments
- Select the most suitable category/categories
- Evaluate the effectiveness of the target segment(s)

iii. Market Research Process

Market research is about understanding a market to which a purposeful and effective planning is required. It has some processes which are as follows:

- Identify the target market segment
- Understand the detail features of the product
- Understand consumer behaviour of the target segment
- Evaluate internal and external business environmental factors of the organisation
- Make a critical assessment
- Derive conclusions and offer recommendations

iv. Communication Process

Promoting products is one of the significant objectives of marketing activity to which effective communication is required. It is equally necessary to communicate with key stakeholders of the organisation, including employees, customers, public, media, and many more. To make an effective communication, an organisation can use the following communication process:

- Ensure the use of qualified message senders
- Select the most effective communication channel (internet, telemarketing, mobile phone applications, emails, social media, and face to face)
- Encode a lucid message and send it through the selected channel(s)
- Understand whether the receiver has correctly decoded the message or not
- Make changes in the process if there is deviation of the message while reaching to the receiver(s)

v. Market Growth Process

Market growth is necessary to expand the size of any business and increase profitability. It is not merely understood as the expansion in geographical area; it is equally understood as increasing the number of customers. An organisation can follow specific processes to grow the market, and they are listed below:

- Identify market growth needs
- Evaluate infrastructure to sustain the market growth
- Determine market growth strategy (market development, market penetration, product development and diversification - Ansoff matrix)
- Apply the selected approach in practice

- Evaluate the effectiveness of the market growth in fulfilling strategic objectives of the organisation
- Bring changes as required to sustain the growth

B. Indirect Marketing Related Process

There are some business processes which are indirectly related to market growth process, and they are - product development process, supply chain management process, selection and recruitment process and strategy development process.

i. Product Development Process

Every business organisation sells products (goods and services) to the target customers. Different organisations might be selling various products to fulfil the needs and desires of the target customers. It is imperative to say that there is a significant role of the product development process to succeed an organisation in fulfilling strategic objectives because it determines products and its quality. If the products are not suitable for the market, it will be complicated for any organisation to succeed in its mission (Annacchino, 2003). An organisation can follow some specific processes to develop the most suitable products, and those processes are:

- Select a target market
- Understand customers' needs/problems
- Review the competitors
- Design products to address particular needs/problems
- Test product(s) in the sample market
- Make necessary changes if required
- Produce products and launch in the market

ii. Supply Chain Management

To produce the product and supply to the end-users, an organisation uses supply chain management (Kahn, 2006) which follows the following processes:

- Outsource/manage raw material
- Process raw material from warehouse or production area
- Store the finished products in the suitable storage
- Transport the products to retailers or shops
- Sell to the end-users

iii. Selection and Recruitment Process

Through the means of selection and recruitment process, an organisation hires employees. Right people should be in the right positions to succeed an organisation in fulfilling marketing objectives (Dale, 2003). For an effective recruitment and selection, an organisation can follow specific processes which are as follows:

- Realise job vacancy
- Analyse and describe job
- Attract as many as possible candidates
- Screen applications
- Interview candidates
- Select and appoint candidates
- Organise induction and training
- Evaluate employees' performance

iv. Strategy Development Process

An organisation should develop effective strategies to be successful in the competitive market environment. According to Etzel (2007), a strategy is the method or framework that shapes the activities of an organisation. It makes an organisation easy to compete in the market. If there is no proper strategy, then objectives cannot be fulfilled. Every organisation tries to develop the most suitable strategy, but most of them become failure because it is not an easy job. It requires much time, effort and expertise. To develop an effective strategy, an organisation has to follow specific processes which are:

- Analyse internal and external business environmental factors
- Understand product features
- Understand consumer behaviour
- Develop an organisation's aims, objectives, visions and mission statement
- Evaluate possible strategies
- Select the most suitable policy
- Use the chosen approach in practice and collect feedback
- Make perpetual improvement to fit in the changing market

3.4.7. Physical Evidence

Physical evidence is also an essential factor of the marketing mix. It helps customers to be convinced or relied on the brand. Further, it underpins to incorporate the right elements to attract and retain more customers. A marketing executive tries to show physical evidence as the signal of reliability of the brand. It is imperative to say that services do not have tangible physical evidence, but a marketing executive tries to design physical cues that create brand identity. Many people make a buying decision based on physical evidence because it bears the quality, validity, credibility and reliability of the product. It can be studied by dividing into four types: physical environment, ambience, spatial layout and cues.

A. Physical Environment

Physical environment is the surroundings of the business organisation, which includes building, parking, furniture, decoration, layout of the showroom, location and space. Any tangible thing that has a physical existence, and is used to operate a business organisation can be understood as the physical environment. It is imperative to say that organisations might have different physical environments due to their specific product, target market, financial capital and others. For example, a corner shop's physical environment and Tesco Extra's physical environments have vast difference due to the size of their target market and product ranges.

B. Ambience

Ambience is the overall atmosphere that includes temperature, smell, colour and sound. It contributes to make a unique brand identity. Further, it adds value to the products and enhances customer experience. A marketing executive focuses on matching ambience with the product (Blythe, 2009). For example, ambience of the hospital is quiet, normal temperature, clinical smell and mostly white colour. If the ambience of the hospital is not appropriate, it negatively affects service users' experience and reduces brand value.

C. Spatial Layout

Spatial layout refers to the ways of arranging furniture and machinery. Different size, shape and level of the furniture and machinery contribute in arousing special effect on customers. For example, furniture's size, shape and spacing help to increase satisfaction of the customers in a restaurant because it helps them to feel comfortable and relaxed. If the spatial layout is not suitable, merely product cannot increase brand value because customers do not enjoy eating at that place. As an organisation cannot attract new and retain existing customers, it cannot achieve competitive advantage.

D. Cues

Cues are signs or symbols that create organisation's particular identity. Colours, logos images and others contribute to make a specific image of the organisation. As there is a sandal brand in Nepal called "Elephant Stamp Sandal" in which elephant is the symbol of strength. Customers believe that it should be as stronger sandal as the strength of the elephant. In the advertisement, it says that there is similarities in strengths between the sandal and elephant. Cues help to make a particular image of the brand or product. And after making a specific image, it allows customers to remind the brand quickly. For example, customers have a kind of good image of the iPhone. As soon as they see its logo, it directly connects customers to its features like iSO, security system, quality service, better camera and other attributes.

3.5. Effective Planning

One of the imperative roles of the management is to develop a planning that should ensure optimum outcomes through the available resources. If any organisation is operating in the competitive market environment without any plan, it cannot sustain for the long term. According to Ruhe (2010), planning is a system that forms organisation culture and offers a clear direction to reach the target. It makes every business activity crystal clear, and the employees can confidently work following the planning.

A proper planning should be clear about objectives, target markets, products, suppliers, financial resources, costs, recruitment and selection methods, machineries, and so on. Developing an effective planning is equal to completing half job. As planning is formulated, everything will be clear, and the rest of the activities are merely executing planning into action. If the planning is not practical, no matter how effective the performance, an organisation cannot sustain in the competitive market environment. It tries to clarify that to succeed in the competitive market, effective planning is inevitable.

A management team has to spend much time to develop a planning because it has to evaluate both internal and external business environmental factors, competitive forces, consumer behaviour and potentiality of the products. Based on these factors, the most suitable aspects should be determined and covered by the planning. It is notable to say that planning should not be firm because the market is in a perpetual changing motion and to accommodate it, changes may be required, which makes planning more effective and efficient. The management should consider the following steps while creating an effective planning:

- Evaluate internal and external business environmental factors

- Assess available resources
- Develop SMART goals
- Identify strategies to achieve the goals
- Determine action plan
- Review planning as per required

3.6. Execution of Planning

Planning is the guideline, and until it is transformed into an action, there is no impact on an organisation's performance. Execution is a careful and logical performance, and it is equally important in every activity to meet the goal (Nash, 2000). Many entrepreneurs have a fantastic idea which are scripted in the planning, but they fail to execute in the performance effectively; thereby, they cannot be successful. Planning is a theory; it merely develops a guideline to meet strategic objectives of an organisation. And execution is a tool that applies approach and performs activities. Appropriate tools are required to implement planning into action effectively; thereby, execution can also be considered as one of the critical aspects of the business organisation.

The core aspects of execution are people, infrastructures, management, and the effectiveness of these factors. People are the employees of the organisation, who use resources, make decision, evaluate performance level, and so on. If people are qualified, experienced, motivated and dedicated, of course, value can be added into execution of the planning. Execution can be equally affected by infrastructures of the organisation. Infrastructures should be supportive or suitable, and they should be mentioned in the planning. If there is no proper infrastructure, performance cannot meet the target objectives, and planning cannot be successful. And there is an equal role of management or leadership to execute planning into performance effectively. Management should use suitable leadership approach, make the right decision, manage necessary infrastructures, assess the quality of the performance, and many more. While executing planning, following points could be considered:

- Be clear about execution objectives
- Have a deeper understanding of the planning
- Have strong will power
- Communicate with key stakeholders
- Participate employees in the decision-making process
- Consult with experts if required
- Systematise the work
- Be punctual and optimistic
- Sharpen management's focus
- Balance on management's point of view
- Take action as the passion
- Keep on continue in monitoring performance and giving advice

3.7. Use of Stakeholders' Feedback

A business organisation has different stakeholders, including employees, customers, suppliers, government, investors, and so on, who have their interests. An organisation has to address those different interests to sustain in the competitive market environment. Ignoring any stakeholder cannot effectively function an organisation's activities. For example, if the customers are not happy with the products, the organisation cannot sell its products, and it cannot achieve target revenue, profitability, brand value, share value, and reputation in the market.

Stakeholders' feedback can be directly related to the performance of the organisation. Every organisation has to collect feedbacks and seriously address them to bring improvement in products and services. It is notable to say that every organisation can have its strengths and weaknesses which can be acknowledged through the means of stakeholders' feedback (Simerson, 2011). Due to this type of feedback, management can make the right decision which might be the key to sustain an organisation in the competitive market environment. Further, it improvers relationship between organisation and stakeholders; it increases product quality, and it satisfies customers' needs. An organisation might have several benefits of using stakeholders' feedback, and they are:

- It helps to find out the organisation's strengths and weaknesses
- It allows opportunities to eradicate flaws on time which stops severe damage on brand identity
- It helps to understand and satisfy the needs and desires of different stakeholders
- It supports management's decision-making process
- It can be used as the tool to enhance the relationship between organisation and stakeholders
- It motivates managerial body and employees to improve their performance
- It helps to bring necessary changes in the organisation to sustain the business for a long term

3.8. Research and Development

Research and Development (R&D) is the process of developing new products or features than that have been existing in the market. It either develops entirely new products or brings some innovative improvements in the existing products. To deliver creative goods and services, at first, the organisation has to spend much time, effort and money in the research process. It is not an easy task because it has to be something special and fulfil customers' needs in a better way. In the competitive market environment, every organisation wants to achieve competitive advantage by using different strategies and out of which differentiation is one of the essential strategies (Porter, 1985). Differentiation rely on R&D, which means to say that by offering innovative goods or services, an organisation can earn extra leverage. If the product is available elsewhere, customers do not retain on a particular brand. But, if the product is available only at a single organisation and it better fulfils customers' needs and desires, it can easily attract new customers and retain the existing. It can sell the products at a premium price as well. It is imperative to say that R&D is equally important all of the time because it should be continued to address the increasing needs and desires of the customers (Laws, 2003). Some of the products related to the technology have a very short product life, and they are aggressively competing through innovativeness. In this type of industry, if the organisation stops its R&D process, the business cannot sustain for a long term. The Smartphone industry has been continuously using new technology; so, to continue the business, every mobile phone companies need to bring something new. Apple Inc. company started to develop iPhone in 2007, but after that, it has provided continuously innovative Smartphone in different versions to arouse the interest and attract more customers. If it did not continue its R&D after releasing the first version, the product lifestyle would be ended, and it would not sustain in the competitive market by this time. But, Nokia could not bring innovation to satisfy its customers; so, it lost the market share. Innovation moves in a particular cycle which involves: synthesising information, data presentation and hypothesising, data analysis, and design, develop, test and improvement (figure 14).

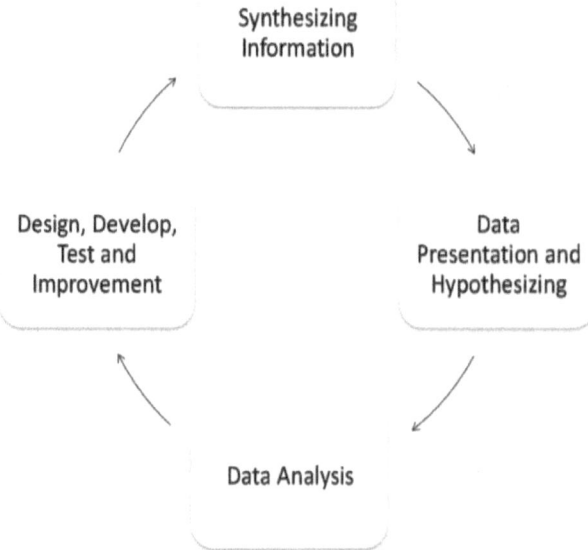

Figure 14: Research and development cycle

3.8.1. Synthesising Information

There is an essential role of data in any R&D practice. Different data might be collected from various data collection instruments, but all of those data should be combined, which is called information synthesising process. This process systematically records every data; so that, the trend of the data can be easily identified.

3.8.2. Data Presentation and Hypothesizing

Raw information is not adequate to conclude any problem; thereby, after collecting information, they must be systematically presented, which may include categorising, tabulating and figuring out. In the course of data presentation, a trend or pattern of the data has to be identified, which is called hypothesising (Hillman and Loewenstein, 2015). Hypothesis is a premature conclusion that is not final; it is merely an assumption which can be rejected or accepted by the findings. But it helps the researcher to concentrate on the critical concerns without deviating from the main issue. It is imperative to say that every research may not require to develop a hypothesis. For example, in qualitative research, formulating hypothesis is not necessary because it uses inductive research approach which follows from particular to general.

3.8.3. Data Analysis

After the data presentation stage, a researcher has to analyse the collected information using suitable data analysis process. There are numbers of data analysis processes as such interpretation, description, compare and contrast, t-test, correlation analysis and many more. Every data analysis process may not be equally suitable for every R&D; thereby, only appropriate one should be selected. It helps to determine the most suitable product(s).

3.8.4. Design, Develop, Test and Improvement

Base on data analysis, the researcher comes across a particular conclusion, which can be a significant insight for designing and developing the product. It guides the production department to determine the most suitable product. As it is new product or feature, the market response is unknown; so, before launching the product in the market, it has to be tested in the sample market and make necessary improvements based on the feedback.

3.9. Perpetual Changes

Any rigid organisation to its strategies and policies cannot sustain for a long term in the competitive market environment because a business is for customers but not for its own. Customers' needs and desires are in constant change, and in the market, competitors keep on entering into the industry with new technology and strategy to gain market share (Kotler and Armstrong, 2008). They try to attract new customers by fulfilling their needs in a better or more effective way. In this situation, any orthodox organisation cannot fit in the market; so, it disappears from the competition as said by Darwin's existential theory. For example, if the customers are interested in buying products from online stores, physical stores have to change their dependency over physical stores. Currently, numbers of retailers like Tesco, Morrison, TK Maxx, Sports Direct and many more are operating both online and physical stores, but they were primarily physical stores. It tries to say that as per the changing situation, a business organisation should also bring necessary changes. An organisation can make changes in different aspect like design of the product, price, quality, service, place, delivery service, warranty and others. But the primary thing is that the changes should better fulfil customers' needs and desires.

3.10. Adequate Financial Resources

Every organisation needs sufficient financial resources to bring necessary changes in business activities. To change product features, update new technology, apply different marketing tools, train employees, and many more, financial resources are necessary. In the lack of sufficient fund, an organisation cannot produce the products to meet the target customers' needs and desires. For example, if the customers want to buy a variety of dairy product, the dairy store must have those varieties. If a dairy store is selling only limited product portfolios in the lack of financial resources, the customers do not buy from that store because they want to buy all of the varieties from a single store. So, such organisation cannot sustain in the competitive market environment.

CHAPTER 4

Business Growth and Develop

4.1. Thrive Objectives

Objectives are the targets of an organisation, which are supported by the strategic performance. Success does not come all of a sudden as a lottery; it is the outcome long term skilful effort. If an organisation wants to grow its business, first of all, it should develop SMART objectives to guide each activity (Nazarko, 2004). Without any purpose, organisation's performance cannot ensure the growth. Also, no planning is possible in the absence of objectives. Thriving objectives is the most vital task to grow or develop a business organisation.

Thriving objective motivates key stakeholders to succeed the business organisation. Ownership of the targets can also be equally important because if the stakeholder do not own it, they cannot be motivated to fulfil those objectives and their performance may not be supportive. As soon as the objectives are developed, it should be well communicated, and a clear roadmap/strategy should be formulated for the organisation's growth.

Objectives should be developed based on a particular framework. There are numbers of tools, but SMART tool is the most reliable and highly being used in business research sector. This tool contributes to secure five critical features of objectives: specific, measurable, achievable, relevant and time-bound (Nazarko, 2004). Business growth goal should be specific instead of a vague or general statement. If it is not accurate, it does not help to motivate employees and to support for developing a growth planning. It means to say that without a specific plan, business growth cannot be systematically carried out. Likewise, growth objective should be measurable. Based on the objectives growth performance should be controlled and monitored. If it is not measurable, the progress cannot be followed, and the performance can be deviated from the target. Likewise, the objective should be achievable; so that, it can have positive impacts on the performance. Similarly, if the objective is not achievable, there is no difference between developing or not developing target. An unachievable goal can be itself an obstacle for the performance, and it cannot be possible to accomplish by applying any strategy. Next, the objective should be highly relevant. The stakeholders have to realise that the targets are relevant for business growth, but if they do not find the relevancy of the objectives, they do not want to fulfil it. And objective should be time-bound which means that it should have a time limit of accomplishing objective. It helps to monitor the progress because the progress can be calculated to find out whether the activities are being performed on the right speed or not. If any objective does not have time-bound, it is difficult to monitor the pace of the performance. Any imprecise time-bound goal can be vague, and it can take a long time to accomplish, which reduces its effectiveness and increases cost and effort.

4.2. Growth Strategies

After sustaining a business, an investor tries to grow it further. Developing a business is not an easy job as it requires adapting suitable growth strategy which can be determined by market research. There are two sectors of business growth: market and product to which Igor Ansoff (1957) has divided into four categories (market penetration, market development, product development and diversification) which are known as Ansoff Matrix (figure 15).

	Existing Products	New Products
Existing Market	Market Penetration	Product Development
New Market	Market Development	Diversification

Figure 15: Ansoff matrix

4.2.1. Market Penetration

Market penetration defuses the existing market with existing products. It is a low-risk strategy because the market and the response to the products are well known. An organisation presents itself in the market more aggressively through various sales campaigns that contributes to increase the use of product in the existing market. It skims market to find all potential customers' needs and desires. Based on the research, it offers different sales promotions to the relevant target customers to attract them at store (Ansoff, 1957). As it increases numbers of customers and sales, the market share will be increased.

4.2.2. Market Development

Market development indicates to the developing new market with the existing products. It does not make any changes in the current products, but it enters into unexplored market. The organisation does not have any insight of the market; thereby, it is challenging to assume whether the existing products can fulfil the market needs and desires or not. In this regard, it has a high risk to be failure (Ansoff, 1957). It seeks low price-conscious market where it sells the product either through new distribution channel(s) or opening new outlet(s). As this is an emerging market, customers do not have other options; thereby, the organisation can have an opportunity to increase the number of new customers with favourable products. This strategy can add a new market segment or an entirely new geographical market, but it should be novel than the existing market.

4.2.3. Product Development

Product development is the condition of selling new product(s) in the existing market. As it is going to sell new products in the well-known market, it will not have that much risk. According to Ansoff (1957), the organisation knows consumer behaviour of its market and such insight helps it to develop the most suitable products. To develop an entirely new product, the organisation requires to invest a significant amount. If the organisation becomes able to develop an innovative product and that satisfy customers' needs and desires, it can have a competitive advantage (Porter, 1985). But when the products become unsuccessful to meet customers' needs and desires, this strategy becomes failure.

4.2.4. Diversification

Diversification growth strategy is the condition of entering into the new market with new product(s). It is the most complicated and riskiest strategy, but it embeds the highest level of potentiality as well. As the market is new, it is tough to understand consumer behaviour and produce the most suitable products (Ansoff, 1957. Developing new products itself is a challenging job, and besides, the market is also unique. In this condition, this strategy is not easy. But as the organisation becomes able to sell the products, it can develop the market as a niche market through which it can achieve a sustainable competitive advantage. This strategy gives higher flexibility to the organisation as it can select the most suitable product and market. Through the help of an intensive research, an organisation can determine the most appropriate market and product.

4.3. Growth Monitoring

As growth planning is implemented into action, the management requires to monitor it to ensure every activity is in the right track to fulfil growth objectives. Quality, quantity, time, cost, and many more aspects should be continuously monitored throughout the implementation process, which helps organisation to find out whether the activities have been following the planning or not (Wilson and Bates, 2005). If some flaws are found in the process, can be eradicated on time; so that, the growth objectives can be easily fulfilled. It means to say that the significant role of growth monitoring is to ensure each activity has been performing correctly or the planning has been effectively implementing. While monitoring growth, following aspects should be considered:

A. Identify the vital elements of the performance to be measured
B. Recognise the importance to measure the particular performance
C. Collect the most suitable data
D. Identify the most appropriate tool to analyse data
E. Assign monitoring responsibility to specific employee or department
F. Determine the authority to report the performance
G. Provide advice, guidance, training and other supports if required
H. Offer feedback and make decisions

4.4. Sustaining the Business Growth

Most of the business organisations have a primary objective to grow and develop. To grow a company, it requires lots of aspects including adequate infrastructure, qualified and dedicated human resources, latest technology, effective strategy, careful market research and selection of proper products/services (Latif, 2010). Business culture should firmly accommodate the changes to sustain the growth. If confusion remains while adapting new systems and strategies, growth foundation might be affected, and problems might arouse in the sustainability of the growth. Inconsistence in business operation, lack of finance to manage infrastructure, high staff turnover rate, ineffective leadership and management, and lack of continuous market research can be some of the imperative barriers in sustainability of the business growth. Workplace culture or business foundation can be an essential factor as it contributes to increase employees' dedication and motivation. Until and unless the growth is not systematised or established as organisational culture, growth cannot sustain for the long term. According to Llopis (2015), six key factors contribute to develop a strong foundation for the growth sustainability. And they are - employees' talent, effective and efficient operation, right target market, right decision on right time, great leadership and risk-taking power.

4.4.1. Employees' Talent

The role of human resource is significant in the growth and sustainability of an organisation. If the employees are capable of performing their roles and responsibilities, the growth can be easier and sustainable (Llopis, 2015). The concept of right people in the right position better clarifies how an organisation has to manage its employees to succeed in achieving competitive leverage. Only the right employees can produce quality products and offer standard services that fulfil the needs and desires of the target market. Lack of the required talent increases operation cost, time and effort. In this regard, to sustain the growth, an organisation has to give much more focus on developing talent.

4.4.2. Effective and Efficient Operation

Effective operation is related to developing quality products, whereas efficient operation is associated with saving cost through the means of quick and accurate performance with no wastage of material. Producing the most suitable product at low cost can be understood as an effective and efficient operation which is one of the critical pillars of sustainable growth (Llopis, 2016). It ensures business operation's particular configuration with business growth and its sustainability.

The business organisation should adopt effective and efficient operation as the business culture because it is the foundation of success.

4.4.3. Selection of Right Target Market

A business organisation might have particular attributes which can satisfy a specific market. If it selects the right target market, it will be easy to meet the market needs and demands. For example, if a cafe shop sells tasty tea to the tea-loving market segment, the customers can be satisfied, and organisation can be successful. But if it selects coffee-loving market segment, neither the customers can be happy, nor the organisation can be successful. In this regard, until and unless an organisation chooses the right market, the growth cannot sustain.

4.4.4. Right Decision at Right Time

A business leader or manager has to make several decisions while running a business organisation. If those decisions are appropriate, they help the organisation to succeed in fulfilling strategic objectives. The decision should make an alignment with growth and its sustainability, but if they contradict each other, no growth will sustain. To make the right decision at the right time, a leader or manager should have decision-making skills and abilities. A leader with vision, dedication, risk-taking ability, appropriate qualification and experience can make a better decision (Llopis, 2015). Right timing and depth knowledge about subject matter can also be equally essential to make the right decision.

4.4.5. Great Leadership

Some people might have innate leadership qualities, and if they get the right environment, they can be great leaders. A great leader can make the right decision, have excellent vision, devise proper strategy, and monitor the progress. She/he might have long term planning that does not let the growth down. Further, such leaders can have a strong immune to work in high pressure without losing control. According to House et al. (2004), if an organisation has strong leadership, each activity can be directed to the right direction. And the growth can be sustainable for the long term. As per the growth essence, she/he can lead each business activity by making the right decision, motivating employees, developing proper planning and adequately monitoring the performance.

4.4.6. Risk-Taking Ability

Every opportunity or success comes along with risk, and if a leader does not want to take risk, she/he might miss opportunities. A manager always tries to reduce risk, but a leader tries to take it; so, risk-taking is the leadership quality which is equally required in the manager as well. Every new decision may not have a hundred per cent certainty of success as it has not been previously tested. Some people can be afraid of risk-taking, and they cannot bring any new changes; instead they want to stick on the existing business system and operation. If they do not want to take any risk, business activities do not support the growth.

In addition to the above mentioned six factors, the following aspects should also be equally considered to sustain the business growth:

- A. Adequate financial resources
- B. Good working environment
- C. Employees' participation in the decision-making process
- D. Stakeholders' feedback
- E. Perpetual market research
- F. Selection of effective strategies

A. Adequate Financial Resources

Business growth indicates the expansion of market or/and product to which an organisation requires extra financial capital. It may need to arrange new infrastructures, more raw materials, additional buildings, new technology and extra-human resources. In the lack of adequate financial resources, the organisation cannot manage those aspects, and the growth cannot sustain for the long term. Before growth or development of the business, the organisation has to calculate the potential extra cost for the growth sustainability and manage suitable source(s); so that, the growth will not be discontinued in the lack of financial resources.

B. Good Working Environment

As the employees are trained, satisfied and helpful to each other, their performance can be better. Participating them in the decision-making process increases ownership of the decision and motivates to support it. And teamwork helps them to learn new skills and abilities from the co-workers. Employees are the key stakeholders of any business organisation as they directly involve in producing products or offering services by employing other resources. In this regard, they should be given an excellent environment to sustain the growth. If the working environment is upsetting, they cannot explore their optimum potentiality, and the growth cannot adequately sustain for the long term.

C. Employees' Participation in Decision Making

As mentioned already, employees' participation in the decision-making process is essential to sustain the business growth. If they are actively participated in the decision-making process, they believe that the organisation values them. Moreover, they own the decision, and they try to give their best performance to succeed the decision.

D. Stakeholders' Feedback

For the growth sustainability, an organisation may require a continuous change in different aspects of the operation based on the stakeholders' feedback. Same types of products, strategies, promotions, processes and others may not be suitable in the changing situation. Customers' needs and desires, market competition and external business environmental factors can be rapidly chaining and to fit with those changes, an organisation has to bring some changes. While bringing changes, stakeholders' feedback can be prominent as they can provide the factual information that helps to sustain the growth.

E. Perpetual Market Research

Continuous market research increases knowledge about the market, which helps an organisation to develop a proper planning and tackle with any obstacle of the growth sustainability. Competitors' situation, economic situation of the target market, changing needs and desires, and the market perception over the products and services can be updated if there is a continuous market research. It helps an organisation to bring quick improvements in mistakes. As customers build up a negative image, it will be tough to change such image. A market research sketches overall map of the market and helps to develop the most suitable strategies to sustain the growth.

F. Effective Strategies

The more an organisation has effective strategies, the more it can be successful. Effective strategies are the keys to success as they show a clear roadmap to achieve the objectives. Most of the business organisations grow and develop their businesses, but only a few of them become able to sustain for a long time. As per the nature of the products or services, different organisations might require different types of strategies. And the selection of those strategies may depend upon specific attributes and quality of the particular organisation.

REFERENCES

Abdul, Y. (2009). *The Art of Islamic Banking and Finance: Tools and Techniques for Community-Based Banking.* New Jersey: John Wiley and Sons.

Adu, P. (2019). *A Step-by-step Guide to Qualitative Data Coding.* London: Routledge.

Agarwal, R. (1982). *Organisation and Management.* New Delhi: Tata McGraw-Hill Publishing Company Limited.

Allen, R. (2009). *The British Industrial Revolution in Global Perspective.* Cambridge: Cambridge University Press.

Amatori, F. and Colli, A. (2013). *Business History: Complexities and Comparison.* London: Routledge.

Amatori, F. and Jones, G. (eds.) (2003). *Business History around the World.* Cambridge: Cambridge University Press.

Andrei, L. (2011). *Money and Market in the Economy of All Times.* New York: Xlibris Corporation.

Angel, J. F., Kollat, D. T. and Blackwell B. D. (1968) *Consumer Behaviour,* Illinois: Dryden Press.

Ansoff, I. (1957). "Strategies for Diversification," *Harvard Business Review.* Vol. 35(5).

Apple Inc. (2019). "Compare iPhone Models," [Online] Available at https://www.apple.com/uk/iphone/compare/, Accessed on 7th January 2019.

Araya, D. (2018). *Augmented Intelligence: Smart Systems and the Future of Work and Learning.* London: Peter Lang.

Argenti, P. (2012). *The Fast Forward MBA Pocket Reference*. London: John Wiley and Sons.

Armstrong, M. (2006). *A Handbook of Human Resource Management Practice* (10th ed.) London: Kogan Page.

Armstrong, M., Adam, S. and Denize, S. (2014). *Principles of Marketing*. Melbourne: Pearson.

Asifulla, A. (2016). *Introduction to Electronic Banking*. New Delhi: Educreation Publication.

Bailey, D. and Chapain, C. (2012). *The Recession and Beyond: Local and Regional Response to the Downtown*. London: Routledge.

Baker, R. (2010). *Implementing Value Pricing: A Radical Business Model for Professional Firms*. London: John Wiley and Sons.

Baker, R. (2017). *Measure What Matters to Customers*. London: John Wiley and Sons.

Bazeley, P. and Jackson, K. (eds.) (2013). *Qualitative Data Analysis With NVivo*. London: SAGE.

Beaver, A. (2005). *A Dictionary of Travel and Tourism Terminology*, Oxon: GABI Publishing.

Belk, R. (1982). "Acquiring Processing and Collecting: Fundamental Processes in Consumer Behaviour," in Ronald F. Bush and Shelby G. Hunt (eds.) *Marketing Theory: Philosophy of Science Perspective*. Chicago: American Marketing Association.

Bhat, S. (2008). *Financial Management: Principles and Practice* (2nd ed.). New Delhi: Excel Books.

Blackford, M. (2012). *The Rise of Modern Business*. North Carolina: The University of North Carolina Press.

Blackwell, D. R., Miniard, P. W. and Engel J. F. (2006) *Consumer Behaviour* (10th ed.). Mason: South-Western.

Blythe, J. (2009). *Key Concepts in Marketing*. London: SAGE Publications Ltd.

Boobyer, C. (2003). *Leasing and Asset Finance: The Comprehensive Guide for Practitioners*. (4th ed.). London: Euromoney Books.

Boone, L. and Kurtz, D. (2014). *Contemporary Marketing*. London: CENGAGE Learning.

British Museum (2017). "The Industrial Revolution and the Changing Face of Britain" [Online] Available at https://www.britishmuseum.org/research/publications/online_research_catalogues/paper_money/paper_money_of_england__wales/the_industrial_revolution/the_industrial_revolution_3.aspx, Accessed on 5th November 2018.

Broadbent, M. and Cullen, J. (2012). *Managing Financial Resources* (3rd ed.). London: Butterworth Heinemann.

Brossman, M. and McGaha, A. (2011). *Social Media for Business.* London: Outer Banks Publishing Group.

Brown, R. (1998). *Honda: The Complete Story.* London: Crowood.

Bryman, A. (2015). *Social Research Methods* (5th ed.). Oxford: Oxford University Press.

Burgan, M. (2013). *The European Industrial Revolution.* London: Scholastic Incorporated.

Burnette, J. (2008). *Gender, Work and Wages in Industrial Revolution Britain.* Cambridge: Cambridge University Press.

Careers, R. (2018). *Inbound Sales Representative.* London: CreateSpace.

Carmichael, D. and Graham, L. (2012). *Accountants' Handbook, Special Industries and Special Topics.* New Jersey: John Wiley and Sons.

Cash, P., Stankovic, T. and Storga, M. (eds.) (2016). *Experimental Design Research.* Zurich: Springer.

Ceruzzi, P. and Aspray, W. (2003). *A History of Modern Computing* (2nd ed.). London: The MIT Press.

Cheock, J. (2017). *China Myth or History.* Beijing: Cheok.

Chikuhwa, J. (2013). *Business Management.* IN: AuthorHouse.

Cipolla, C. (2004). *Before the Industrial Revolution* (3rd ed.). London: Routledge,

Clark, J. (2004). *Railroads in the Civil War.* New York: LSU Press.

Clow, K. and Stevens, C. (2009). *Concise Encyclopaedia of Professional Services Marketing.* London: Routledge.

Conkin, P. (2008). *A Revolution Down on the Farm.* New York: University Press of Kentucky.

Cook, S. (2004). *Measuring Customer Service Effectiveness.* London: Gower.

Coyle, B. (2002). *Bank Finance*. London: Financial World Publishing.

Crone, P. (2015). *Pre-industrial Societies: Anatomy of the Pre-Modern World*. London: One World Publications.

Cronin, M. (ed.) (1998). *Banking and Finance on the Internet*. New York: John Wiley and Sons.

Culey, S. (2018). *Transition Point*. London: Matador.

Dahotre, N. and Harimkar, S. (2008). *Laser Fabrication and Machining of Materials*. TN: Springer Science and Business.

Davenport, T. (2018). *The AI Advantage*. London: The MIT Press.

Davies, G. (2010). *History of Money*. Cardiff: University of Wales Press.

Dent, J. (2008). *Distribution Channels: Understanding and Managing Channels to Market*. London: Kogan Page.

Dent, J. and White, M. (2018). *Sales and Marketing Channels: How to Build and Manage Distribution Strategy*. London: Kogan Page.

Dibb, S. and Simkin, L. (2008). *Market Segmentation Success*. London: Routledge.

Dibb, S. and Simkin, L. (2012). *Marketing Briefs: A Revision and Study Guide*. Oxford: Butterworth-Heinemann.

Dixon, J., Gibbon, D. and Gulliver, A. (2001). *Farming Systems and Poverty: Improving Farmers' Livelihoods in a Changing World*. Washington DC: FAO and World Bank.

Dlabay, L. and Burrow, J. (2007). *Business Finance*. London: Thomson.

Dolnicar, S., Grun, B. and Leisch, F. (2018). *Market Segmentation Analysis*. Oberosterreich: Springer.

Doran, T. (1981). "There's a SMART Way to Write Management's Goals and Objectives," *Management Review*. Vol. 70, Issue 11, Pp. 35-36.

Dosi, G. and Galambos, L. (eds.) (2013). *The Third Industrial Revolution in Global Business*. Cambridge: Cambridge University Press.

Dransfield, R. (2005). *Applied Business*. London: Heinemann.

Dris, R. and Jain, M. (eds.) (2007). *Quality Handling and Evaluation*. New York: Kluwer Academic Publishers.

Drucker, P. (1955). *The Practice of Management*. London: Heinemann.

Dummies, C. (2009) *Managing Your Money All-in-One for Dummies*, Hoboken: Wiley Publishing Inc.

Egan, J. (2007). *Marketing Communications*. London: Thomson.

Etzel, J. M. (2007). *Marketing* (13th ed.). New Delhi: Tata McGraw-Hill Publishing Company.

Ferrell, O. C. and Hartline, M. (2011). *Marketing Strategy* (5th ed.). Mason: South-Western.

Foley, J. Frerking, R., Hollands, M., Jackson, R., Mathis, K., Wakelin, P and Webster, M. (2016). *How Wal-Mart Became a Cloud Service Provider with IBM CICS*. New York: Red Book.

Forbes (2017). "America's Top 50 Companies 1917-2017" [Online] Available at https://www.forbes.com/sites/jeffkauflin/2017/09/19/americas-top-50-companies-1917-2017/, Accessed on, 2nd May 2019.

Frasel, N. and Druce, N. (2006). *Partnership for Malaria Control*. London: World Health Organization.

Gagnier, R. (2018). *Literatures of Liberalization*. London: Palgrave Macmillan.

Gale, N., Heath, G., Cameron, E., Rashid, S. and Redwood, S. (2013). "Using the Framework Method for the Analysis of Qualitative Data in Multi-disciplinary Health Research," *BMC Medical Research Methodology*. Vol. 13(117).

Gard, C. (2002). *The Attack on the Pentagon on September 11, 2001*. New York: The Rosen Publishing Group.

Goddard, L. (2011). *Remembering Marshall Field's*. New York: Arcadia Publishing.

Goloboy, J. (2008). *Industrial Revolution: People and Perspective*. Oxford: ABC CLIO.

Grant, T. (2005). *International Directory of Company Histories*. New York: St. James Press.

Gray, G. and Balmer, J. (1998). "Managing Corporate Image and Corporate Responsibility," *Long Range Planning*. Vol. 5(21).

Greer, M. H. (2010). *A Practitioner's Guide to Class Action*. New York: American Bar Association.

Gregory, A. (2004). *Public Relations in Practice* (2nd ed.). London: Kogan Page.

Groover, M. (2010). *Fundamentals of Modern Manufacturing: Materials, Processes, and Systems* (4th ed.). MA: John Wiley and Sons.

Groucutt, J. (2005). *Foundation of Marketing.* New York: Palgrave Foundation.

Grusky, D., Western, B. and Wimer, C. (eds.) (2011). *The Great Recession.* London: Russell Sage Foundation.

Gubrium, J., Holstein, J., Marvasti, A. and McKinney, K (eds.) (2012). *The SAGE Handbook of Interview Research* (2nd ed.). London: SAGE.

Gupta, S. (2004). *Marketing Research.* New Delhi: Excel Books.

Gupta, S. and Randhawa, G. (2008). *Retail Management.* New Delhi: Atlantic Publishers and Distributors.

Haig, M. (2002). *Mobile Marketing: The Message Revolution.* London: Kogan Page.

Handley, L. (2017). "Half of All Advertising Dollars will be Spent Online by 2020, Equalling all Combined Offline ad Spent Globally," *CNBC.* 4th December 2017.

Harrison, H., Birks, M., Franklin, R. and Mills, J. (2017). "Case Study Research: Foundations and Methodological Orientations," *Qualitative Social Research.* Vol. 18(1).

Hartwell, R. (2017). *The Causes of the Industrial Revolution in England.* London: Routledge.

Hedges, R., Levy, M. and Proud, I. (2007). *The 5 Elements of the Highly Effective Debt Collector.* Bloomington: iUniverse.

Hillman, R. and Loewenstein, M. (eds.) (2015). *Research Handbook on Partnerships.* London: Edward Elgar Publishing Limited.

Hobsbawm, E. (1977). *The Age of Revolution: Europe 1789-1848.* London: Abacus.

Hofacker, C. (2018). *Digital Marketing: Communicating, Selling and Connecting.* London: Edward Elgar Publishing.

Hoffman, K. D. (2005). *Marketing Principles and Best Practices,* (3rd ed.). Mason: South-Western.

Hoover, G. (1992). *Hoover's Handbook of World Business.* London: Reference Press.

House, R., Hanges, P., Javidan, M., Dorfman, P. and Gupta, V. (eds.) (2004). *Culture, Leadership and Organization.* London: SAGE Publications.

Howgego, C. (2002). *Ancient History from Coins.* London: Routledge.

Hunter, M. (2013). "A Short History of Business and Entrepreneurial Evolutions During the 20th Century: Trend for the New Millennium," *Geopolitics, History and International Relations.* Vol. 5(1).

Ingram, T., LaForge, R. and Avila, R. (2012). *Sales Management: Analysis and Decision Making* (8th ed.). New York: M. E. Sharpe.

Jackson, T. and Shaw, D. (2008). *Mastering Fashion Marketing.* London: Macmillan International.

Jeremy, D. (1998). *A Business History of Britain, 1900-1990s.* Oxford: Oxford University Press.

Jethwaney, J. and Jain, S. (2007). *Advertising Management.* (3rd ed.). Oxford: Oxford University Press.

Jha, L. (2008). *Customer Relationship Management: A Strategic Approach.* New Delhi: Global India Publications.

Johnston, J. (2013). *Media Relations: Issues and Strategies* (2nd ed.). London: Allen and Unwin.

Jones, S. (2009). *Business-to-business Internet Marketing* (5th ed.). New York: Maximum Press.

Jones, T. (2015). *Artificial Intelligence.* London: Jones and Bartlett Publishers.

Kerridge, E. (2013). *The Agricultural Revolution.* London: Routledge.

Ketkar, S. and Ratha, E. (eds.) (2008). *Innovative Finance for Development.* New York: The World Bank Publications.

King, S. and Timmins, G. (2001). *Making Sense of the Industrial Revolution.* Manchester: Manchester University Press.

Kirby, P. (2013). *Child Workers and Industrial Health in Britain, 1780-1850.* London: The Boydell Press.

Kolbe, P., Greer, G. and Rudner, G. (2003). *Real State Finance.* Chicago: Dearborn Real Estate Education.

Kotler, P. and Armstrong, G. (2008). *Principles of Marketing* (12th ed.). New Delhi: Pearson Prentice Hall.

Kotler, P., Burton, S., Deans, K., Brown, L. and Armstrong, G. (2015). *Marketing* (9th ed.). NSW: Pearson.

Kumar, N. (2004). *Marketing as Strategy.* Boston: Harvard Business School Press.

Kurtz, D. and Boone, L. (2008). *Contemporary Business* (12th ed.). Mason: South-Western.

Lamb, C., Hair, J. and McDaniel, C. (2008). *Essentials of Marketing* (6th ed.). Mason: South-Western.

Latif, A. (ed.) (2010). *Innovation in Business and Enterprise.* New York: Business Science Reference.

Laudon, K. and Traver, C. (2015). *E-commerce: Business, Technology, Society.* London: Pearson.

Launder, B. (2019). *Build a Thriving Direct Sales Business.* London: Connected Women of Influence.

Laws, S. (2003). *Research for Development: A Practical Guide.* London: SAGE.

Lee, M. and Johnson, C. (2005) *Principles of Advertising: A Global Perspective,* 2nd ed. New York: Haworth.

Lee, R. (2016). *Commerce and Culture: Nineteenth-Century Business Elites.* London: Ashgate Publishing.

Liu, J.(2011). *Supply Chain Management and Transport Logistics.* London: Routledge.

Llopis, G. (2015). "Top 6 Ways to Sustain Business Growth" Fobs. [Online] Available at https://www.forbes.com/sites/glennllopis/2015/09/29/top-6-ways-to-sustain-business-growth/#33dcfc2867ee, Accessed on 22nd December 2018.

Lopus, J. (2013). *Student Handbook to Economics: Microeconomics.* Landisville: EJB Publishing Services.

Loton, D. (2008). *Win Your Way to Wealth: Win Competitions and Sell Your Prizes Online.* London: Lotontech Limited.

Luxemburg, R. (2012). *Reform or Revolution and Other Writings.* New York: Dover Publications.

Machado, C. (ed.) (2013). *Effective Human Resources Management in Small and Medium Enterprises.* PA: IGI Global.

Magnusson, L. (2015). *The Political Economy of Mercantilism.* London: Routledge.

Makdisi, S. (2007). *William Blake and the Impossible History of the 1790s.* Chicago: The University of Chicago.

Maslow, A. (1970). *Motivation and Personality* (2nd ed.). New York: Harper and Row.

Mason, J. (2017). *Qualitative Researching* (3rd ed.). Sage: London.

McBurney, D. and White, T. (2009). *Research Methods*. Belmont: Wadsworth.

McNeese, T. (2002). *The Industrial Revolution*. London: Lorenz Educational Press.

Medina, R. (2006). *Personnel and Human Resources Management* (6th ed.). Manila: Rex Books.

Meyer, S. (2016). *The Neolithic Revolution*. New York: Rosen Publishing.

Middleton, K. (2018). *Competing for Kids*. New York: Wheatmark.

Middleton, V. And Clarke, J. (2012). *Marketing in Travel and Tourism*. Oxford: Butterworth-Heinemann.

Mishra, R. (2009). *Materials Management*. New Delhi: Excel Books.

Mitchell, M. and Jolley, J. (2009). *Research Design Explained* (7th ed.). Belmont: Wadsworth.

Moens, G. (2003). *International Trade and Business Law Review*. London: Cavendish Publishing Limited.

Mohan, M. (1989). *Advertising Management: Concepts and Cases*. New Delhi: Tata McGraw Hill

Mokyr, J. (2018). *The British Industrial Revolution: An Economic Perspective* (2nd ed.). New York: Routledge.

Morris, G., McKay, S. and Oates, A. (2009). *Finance Director's Handbook* (5th ed.). London: Elsevier.

Moustakas, C. (1994). *Phenomenological Research Methods*. London: SAGE.

Mullen, J. and Daniels, D. (2011). *Email Marketing: An Hour a Day*. New Jersey: John Wiley and Sons.

Murthy, S. and Bhojanna, U. (2007). *Advertising*. New Delhi: Excel Books.

Nash, E. (2000). *Direct Marketing: Strategy, Planning, Execution*. London: McGraw Hill.

Nazarko, L. (2004). *Managing a Quality Service*. London: Heinemann Educational Publishers.

Neuendorf, K. (2016). *The Content Analysis Guidebook* (2nd ed.). London: SAGE.

Pailwar, V. (2011). *Economic Environment of Business* (3rd ed.). New Delhi: PHI Learning.

Pandey, I. (2015). *Financial Management* (11th ed.). New Delhi: Vikas Publishing House.

Perreault, D. W. and McCarthy E. J. (2006). *Basic Marketing: A Global Managerial Approach* (5th ed.). New Delhi: Tata McGraw-Hill Publishing Company Limited.

Porter, M. (1985). *Competitive Advantage: Creating and Sustaining Superior Performance*. New York: The Free Press.

Pride, W. and Ferrell, O. (2008). *Foundations of Marketing* (3rd ed.). Boston: Cengage Learning.

Pride, W. M., Hughes, R. J., Kapoor, J. R. (2012). *Business* (11th ed.). Mason: South-Western.

Rao, V. (ed.) (2009). *Handbook of Pricing Research in Marketing*. London: Edward Elgar.

Reynolds, P. and Lancaster, G. (2007). *Marketing Made Simple*. London: Taylor and Francis.

Rigby, G. (2011). *Types and Sources of Finance for Start-up and Growing Businesses*. London: Harriman House Ltd.

Ritchie, J. and Lewis, J. (2003). *Qualitative Research Practice: A Guide for Social Science Students and Researches*. London: Sage.

Roberts, M. and Berger, P. (1999). *Direct Marketing Management* (2nd ed.). New Jersey: Prentice-Hall.

Russell, B. (1984). "A Manifesto for a Consumer Behaviour of Consumer Behaviour," In Anderson Paul F. and Michaela J. Ryan (eds.) *Educators Proceeding*. Chicago: American Marketing Association.

Ruthe, G. (2010). *Product Release Planning: Methods, Tools and Applications*. New York CRC Press.

Ryan, T. and Jacobs, C. (2005). *Using Investor Relations to Maximize Equity Valuation*. New Jersey: John Wiley and Sons.

Sainsbury's Website (2016). "Help Centre Home - Company Values" [Online] Available at https://help.sainsburys.co.uk/help/company-values/donate-to-charity, Accessed on 24th October 2018.

Santucci, R. (2013). *Business Planning for Affordable Housing Development*. New York: Xlibris Corporation.

Saunders, M., Lewis, P. and Thornhill, A. (2009). *Research methods for business students* (5th ed.). Harlow: Prentice-Hall.

Sawant, R. (2010). *Infrastructure Investing*. New Jersey: John Wiley and Sons.

Schaechter, A. (2002). *Issues in Electronic Banking: An Overview*. Washington: International Monetary Fund.

Schmitt, B. (2011). *Experience Marketing*. New York: Now Publishers Inc.

Schultz, B. and Varouxakis, G. (eds.) (2005). *Utilitarianism and Empire*. New York: Lexington Books.

Schumpeter, J. (1950). *Capitalism, Socialism, and Democracy*. London: HarperCollins.

Schwab, K. (2017). *The Fourth Industrial Revolution*. London: Penguin.

Sekaran, U. and Bougie, R. (2016). *Research Methods for Business: A Skill Building Approach*. London: John Wiley and Sons.

Shah, J. (2009). *Supply Chain Management: Text and Cases*. New Delhi: Pearson Education.

Shareef, M., Dwivedi, Y. and Kumar, V. (2016). *Mobile Marketing Channel: Online Consumer Behaviour*. London: Springer.

Shaw, W. and Barry, V. (2015). *Moral Issues in Business* (13th ed.). London: Cengage Learning.

Shimokawa, K. (1994). *The Japanese Automobile Industry: A Business History*. London: The Athlone Press.

Silverberg, D. L. and Cullen, T. A. (2006). *Employer's Guide to Military Leave Compliance* (2nd ed.). London: Thomson.

Simerson, B. (2011). *Strategic Planning: A Practical Guide to Strategy Formulation and Execution*. London: Praeger.

Smith, M., Thorpe, R. and Jackson, P. (2015). *Management and Business Research* (5th ed.). London: SAGE.

Smith, P. and Taylor, J. (2004). *Marketing Communications: An Integrated Approach* (4th ed.). London: Kogan Page.

Smith, T. J. (2011). *Pricing Strategy: Setting Price Levels, Managing Price Discount, and Establishing Price Structure*. Mason: South-Western.

Solomon, M. (2004). *Consumer Behaviour*. London: Pearson Prentice Hall.

Spacey, J. (2017). "7 Types of Public Relations," [Online] Available at https://simplicable.com/new/public-relations, Accessed on 23rd January 2019.

Stanton, N., Salmon, P. and Jenkins, D. (2009). *Human Factors in Design and Evolution of Central Control Room*. London: CRC Press.

Statista (2019). "Global Advertising Spending from 2010 to 2018," [Online] Available at https://www.statista.com/statistics/236943/global-advertising-spending/, Accessed on 16th January 2019.

Stickney, C., Weil, R. and Schipper, K. (2009). *Financial Accounting: An Introduction to Concepts, Methods and Uses*. Mason: South-Western.

Stoltman, J. (2018). *20 Fun Facts about the Industrial Revolution*. New York: Gareth Stevens Publishing.

Stone, L. (ed.) (2013). *An Imperial State at Britain from 1689-1815*. London: Routledge.

Sullivan, M. and Adcock D. (2012) *Retail Marketing*, London: Thomson.

Taylor, S. (2013). *What is Discourse Analysis?* New York: Bloomsbury.

Theaker, A. (2004). *The Public Relations Handbook* (2nd ed.). London: Routledge.

Thmopson, J. and Martin, F. (2005). *Strategic Management: Awareness and Change* (5th ed.). London: South-western.

Thomas, M. J. (1995). *Gower Handbook of Marketing*. Aldershot: Gower Publishing Limited.

Trehan, M. and Trehan, R. (2007). *Advertising and Sales Management*. New Delhi: V.K. Enterprise.

Vareu, R. (2002). *Marketing Communication: Principles and Practices*. London: Routledge.

Venugopal, K. (2006). *Business Economics Volume*. London: New Age International.

Walton, P. and Aerts, W. (2006). *Global Financial Accounting and Reporting: Principles and Analysis*. London: Thomson.

Ward, A. and Sobek, D. (2014). *Lean Product and Process Development* (2nd ed.). MA: Lean Enterprise Institute.

Weatherford, J. (2009). *The History of Money*. New York: Three Rivers Press.

Wilson, J. (1995). *British Business History, 1720-1994*. Manchester: Manchester University Press.

Wilson, J., Toms, S. and Jong, A. (2016). *The Routledge Companion to Business History*. London: Routledge.

Wison, P. and Bates, S. (2005). *The Essential Guide to Managing Small Business Growth*. London: John Wiley and Sons.

Wolfe, J. (2015). *The Industrial Revolution*. New York: Rosen Publishing.

Wood, E. (2002). *The Origin of Capitalism: A Longer View*. London: Verso.

Wrigley, E. (2010). *Energy and the English Industrial Revolution*. Cambridge: Cambridge University Press.

Yeshine, T. (2006). *Sales Promotion*. London: Thomson.

Zhang, J. (2014). *The Tradition and Modern Transition of Chinese Law*. Beijing: Springer.

Zimmerman, A. and Blythe, J. (2017). *Business to Business Marketing Management* (2nd ed.). London: Routledge.

www.ingramcontent.com/pod-product-compliance
Lightning Source LLC
Chambersburg PA
CBHW020654220526
45464CB00001B/432